In recent years  file cases of murders committed... ll illustrate, murder by children is by no means ...menon. Now, as then, we struggle to comprehend, searching our society for the reasons why.

In the aftermath of all murders by children, people desperately sought some sort of explanation, unwillingly to acknowledge that supposedly innocent beings would behave so bestially. In the wake of the murder of Frederick Hughes in 1903 by eight-year-old Patrick Knowles *The Spectator* published an editorial on the matter, asking 'How does it come about that an English boy, at an age when most children think about very little that is not innocent, can have been urged by so devilish an impulse as to take pleasure in the death of a helpless baby?'

The writer acknowledged that many young boys began to display some form of criminal tendencies at the age of fourteen or fifteen - some began to lie; some to steal and others to display cruelty towards animals or other children. Yet, at this age, the body grew faster than the mind, leading to a dominance of a boy's animalistic side. As the maturation of the mind caught up with that of the body, boys tended to become gentler.

Patrick Knowles was clearly an exceptional case, pointed out the editorial. Although he had two parents, he apparently spent most of his life on the streets, supporting himself by selling matches. 'The fact that a young English boy can commit a diabolical murder is an indictment of the community itself' concluded the writer. 'The main fact is that, while it is inconceivable that a child born and brought up under healthy, happy and safe conditions would ever desire to commit murder – what self-respecting English parent would admit that it could be possible for his own child to be guilty of such a crime? A boy born and brought up under other conditions confesses that he has murdered deliberately...What should be done with him, in the light of his propensity to murder?' asked the writer.

The Spectator placed much of the blame on environmental conditions, coupled with '...the miserable education in crime literally enforced on children'. Whole families were crammed into single rooms described as akin to piggeries; there was a lack of proper food, want of air, disregard of any form of cleanliness or proper sanitation, the cursing of the street brawler underneath the windows and, in all probability, a drunken father and mother. 'What chance has the city child born and brought up under conditions such as those of becoming a decent and useful citizen?'

Recognising the impossibility of eradicating slum housing, the newspaper then offered its own solution, proposing that children should be made to take physical exercise in the form of some kind of military drill. 'Compulsory drill means medical inspection' pointed out the writer 'and degeneration in body or mind – the two usually go together – would be detected and, when once it was detected, special measures in special cases could be taken.' The article continued 'Under a thorough form of physical exercise for children in English schools, it might be made impossible for a child afflicted with mania to be at large.'

This view was largely supported by those trying to find reasons for the murder of two young girls in 1921 by Harold Jones. 'Medical men who had a chance to study the boy at his trial in the Shire Hall, Monmouth, are of the opinion that if he had been employed in an open-air job, such as on a farm, he might never have been in his present position. A lad immensely big for his years, the work of a shop boy was more of a luxury life than anything else, with the result that instead of the muscles becoming stronger, the brain was allowed to develop and, in the absence of any guiding principles, unfortunately in the wrong direction.' Having decided that Harold was not insane, while he was imprisoned, it was reported that 'eminent British Scientists' were searching for 'the microbe in the brain' that brought about his terrible murders. Many newspapers described Jones in animalistic terms stating that he was as stubborn as a mule, as vain as a peacock and as strong as a lion and describing the way in which he '…showed his teeth and snarled' from the dock at the prosecutor's words.

'If he were not allowing himself to become intoxicated on the strains from the organ, he was reading all manner of detective stories from the sound and literary ones to the dangerous and trashy cheap ones' reported *The World's Pictorial News*. 'On my soul, I could not help what I did.' Harold later said when interviewed.

In compiling this collection, I need to thank Ana Ramos for her painstaking research on my behalf and, as always, I must thank my husband, Richard, for his help and support throughout.

Every effort has been made to clear copyright; however my apologies to anyone I may have inadvertently missed. I can assure you it was not deliberate but an oversight on my part.

'If it was to do, I would do it again.'

Eyke, Suffolk, 1748.

In 1748, ten-year-old William York lived in the poorhouse in Eyke, Suffolk, where he was forced to share a bed with five-year-old Susan Mayhew. William hated Susan, who was a sulky child, with a habit of soiling their shared bed.

On 13 May 1748, William and Susan quarrelled and he slapped her hard with his open hand. She burst into tears and ran out of the house and William picked up a heavy hook that someone had left lying around and followed, intending to kill her.

Once he got outside, he made the decision that he needed a knife rather than a hook and went back indoors to find one. He caught up with Susan on a dung heap and, having seized her left hand, he ran the knife around her entire wrist, cutting her to the bone. He then threw Susan to the ground and knelt on her, before running his knife around her arm again, this time just above the elbow.

When Susan didn't immediately die, William placed his foot on her stomach and cut her again, circling both her right wrist and her right upper arm. Since Susan was still alive, William retrieved the hook and plunged it into her left thigh until it struck bone. Finally, he hit the little girl three times on her head with the hook.

18th century illustration of William York killing Susan Mayhew
(author's collection)

Once Susan was dead, William's next act was to conceal his deeds. He fetched a pail of water from a ditch and stripped Susan naked, washing all of the blood from her body, which he then buried in the muck heap, smoothing the surface to disguise the fact that it had been disturbed. He carefully checked the ground for spots of blood, which he sluiced away with water. He washed the knife and hook, before taking them back into the workhouse and replacing them where he found them. He hid Susan's clothes and washed the blood off his own garments, then coolly went to the dining room and ate his breakfast.

Susan was quickly missed and a search soon uncovered her body. Naturally, questions were asked of all the inhabitants of the poorhouse and although William initially denied knowing what happened to Susan, it soon became evident that he was not telling the truth. Justice of the Peace John Cornelius arranged for the boy to be taken to the Suffolk County Gaol, where he eventually confessed to having killed Susan because she was sulky, she had fouled their bed but, most of all, because he just didn't like her.

William's confession left the authorities with a dilemma. Here was a boy who was just ten years and five months old, who had confessed to murdering a younger child. By his own admission, the murder was planned beforehand and could not be attributed to a crime of passion, particularly since William had considered the only weapon to hand and decided against using it, making a special trip indoors to find a knife. Not only that, but he had made strenuous efforts to conceal what the contemporary newspapers referred to as '…his astonishing barbarity'. By the law of the land, William had to stand trial for his crime and was therefore ordered to appear before Lord Chief Justice Willes at the Bury-St- Edmunds Assizes.

Lord Chief Justice Willes (author's collection)

In the run up to his trial, William was said to be 'cheerful and quite easy'. When he stood in the dock accused of murder, the contemporary newspapers described him as '...behaving very impudently', telling the court 'If it was to do, I would do it again'. Given York's confession, his devil-may-care attitude and his complete lack of remorse, the jury at his trial had little alternative other than to find him guilty, although they strongly recommended mercy on account of his age. Since the only given penalty for murder at the time was sentence of death, Willes had no choice in determining William's punishment.

The judge pronounced the death sentence, stating that he intended to postpone the actual execution until 10 November 1848 in order to consult with his colleagues. Although the law allowed for the execution of ten-year-old boys and there was a clear need for some form of deterrent, to show children that they couldn't just kill anyone that they didn't like, nobody in authority had the stomach to actually follow through with the extreme penalty and William's execution date was postponed again and again. In 1757, three years after the outbreak of the Seven Years War, William was granted a Royal Pardon by George II, on condition that he joined the navy and served on one of His majesty's warships.

'Don't you think, sir, that he is better off than I am now?'

Strood – Aylesford, Kent, 1831

Robert Taylor of Strood, Kent, normally worked as a tallow chandler but illness had left him fighting poverty. He was allowed the weekly sum of nine shillings as relief from the parish of Aylesford and, on 4 March 1831, he sent his thirteen-year-old son Richard Faulkner Taylor to collect the money on his behalf.

Richard had made the journey several times before, often accompanied by his seven-year-old sister, Mary Ann. However, on this occasion, he set off alone, wearing sou'wester hat, a canvas smock, a blue jacket and waistcoat with a kerchief tied around his neck and brown trousers. Before leaving, he asked his father if he might borrow his knife, as he intended to cut some wood on his way home to make himself a bow and arrow.

Richard arrived safely at Aylesford and was given the money by Relieving Officer George Cutbath. As he always did, Richard tucked the three half crowns, the shilling and the sixpenny piece into a little cloth bag, which he then placed inside one of his mittens for safekeeping.

Whenever Richard had made the journey to Aylesford in the past, he had always arrived home at around three o'clock but, on this occasion, three o'clock came and went, with no sign of him. As it grew later, his parents began searching for him and, when he still hadn't returned home the next morning, Robert Taylor went to Aylesford and established that his son had received the money and had been seen setting off to walk home.

Although the police and the general public searched high and low for any sign of the missing boy, he seemed to have vanished off the face of the earth. Bills were printed advertising his disappearance and a generous reward was offered for information leading to his discovery. Then, on 11 May 1831, a man named John Izzard was walking through a wood on the route between Strood and Aylesford when he happened to glance into a ditch and saw a badly decomposed body. Knowing that Richard Taylor was missing, Izzard went straight to the boy's parents, who rushed to the ditch to see if it was their son. There were worms crawling all over the body and although Richard's face had been eaten away, his hair was as it had been on the day he left home. Robert Taylor instantly recognised his son's clothing and, when the boy's upper garments were pulled back to expose his chest, it revealed Richard's distinctive birthmark, which was shaped like a bunch of currants.

The body was taken to St Margaret's Poor House, where it was examined the next day by surgeons Edward Seaton and J.G. Bryant. The doctors concluded that Richard had died as a result of a wound in his throat, which they believed had been inflicted with a sharp-pointed instrument, such as a knife. Richard's clothes were disarranged, as if he had been in a scuffle and the money that the boy had been carrying was missing.

The police immediately began their enquiries into Richard's death and soon found two people, who stated that they had seen Richard in the company of two boys. One of the witnesses was Henry Lewington, who worked as a warrant officer in the Navy. He told police that, on the afternoon of 4 March, he caught up with Richard on his way to Aylesford and walked a short distance with him. At around one o'clock, he saw Richard again, this time walking in the opposite direction. Now Richard was accompanied by two boys – fourteen-year-old John Any Bird Bell and his twelve-year-old brother James.

When Richard went missing, Lewington had told Robert Taylor that he had seen him with the Bell brothers and Robert went straight to see them. They assured him that they had left Richard by a turnip field, from where he was walking towards the Benham road.

Hearing the news that Richard had been found, Lewington sought out the Bells' father, who worked as a wood cutter and thus spent most of his time in the woods, normally accompanied by his two sons. Lewington told Bell that Richard's body had been located and demanded that he bring his two sons to the nearby public house until a policeman could be summoned. Mr Bell complied and, at the Bell Inn, Lewington handed the boys over to the police constable for Burnham parish. However, the officer could see no reason for detaining the boys and immediately released them.

Yet within days, a rusty white-horn-handled knife was found near to where Richard's body lay. Judged to be the murder weapon, it was known to belong to John Bell and, with this new evidence, the police took Bell and his two sons into custody.

Meanwhile, the inquest on Richard Taylor's death was opened. Richard had already been buried but when it was realised that nobody had searched the dead boy's pockets, it was decided to exhume him. John and James Bell were taken to the graveside and, once the coffin had been opened, James was directed to go into the grave and search the corpse's pockets. He did so without flinching, returning with the knife lent to Richard by his father and a worsted glove. Although James had passed that test, his older brother was reluctant to go anywhere near the body. However, the police laid out some bread and cheese with the murder weapon and told the Bells to help themselves. Although obviously hungry, John refused to touch the knife but once again James showed no such qualms.

Although it was strongly suspected that he was an accessory to murder, there was nothing to tie Mr Bell to Richard Taylor's death and he was released from custody. Under questioning by magistrates James revealed that he had acted as lookout, while his brother stabbed and killed Richard. Knowing that Richard regularly walked back from Aylesford carrying money, the Bells had planned his murder for some time and James admitted that he had been given one shilling and sixpence as his share. Although an accessory to the murder, James was released, while John was taken to Maidstone Gaol. On his way, John admitted that his brother's statement was true. He pointed out a pond where he had washed his victim's blood from his hands and the knife and, as they passed an opening in the woods leading to where the body was found, he remarked to Police Constable Charles Patterson 'That's where I killed the poor boy', adding 'Don't you think, sir, that he is better off than I am now?'

As the journey to Maidstone continued, John Bell gradually revealed more and more details of the murder. He told Patterson that he had lured Richard into the wood and having walked round for some time he sat down and pretended that he was lost. Richard lay down and began to cry because he didn't know his way home, at which John jumped on him and stabbed him in the neck. Although he knew that his victim had money on him, it took John some time to find it, since Richard had clutched it tightly inside the mitten on his left hand.

John Any Bird Bell was committed for trial at the Summer Assizes in Maidstone on a charge of wilful murder, appearing before Mr Justice Gaselee on 29 July 1831.

The first witness was Robert Taylor, who told the court about his son's trip to Aylesford and about the discovery of the boy's body some weeks later. Taylor was distraught and fainted several times as he gave his evidence.

Relieving Officer Cutbath testified that Richard had collected the relief money and Henry Lewington recalled walking part of the way to Aylesford with Richard and seeing him later in the company of the Bell brothers. Another witness named Mary Jones had also seen the three boys together on the afternoon of 4 March.

John Izzard described finding the body, after which surgeons Seaton and Bryant gave medical evidence as to the cause of death.

PC John Toff told the court how he had arrested the Bell brothers, claiming that John Bell had told him before Richard's body was exhumed that his knife would be found in his pocket, a statement that brought an objection from John's defence counsel, Mr Clarkson.

Magistrates clerk George Farrel recalled transcribing John's statement and the boy signing it with his cross. This provoked an argument about whether or not John's statement should be admitted as evidence, prompting Mr Justice Gaselee to leave the court and consult with a colleague, Lord Tenterden, before deciding that the statement should be heard. In it, John made a full confession, telling the magistrates 'It was I that did the murder and while I was doing it Jem [James] watched at the back.' John claimed that the knife he used to kill Richard belonged to James and he had borrowed it specifically to cut Richard's throat and steal his money. 'The boy squeaked when his throat was cut as a rabbit squeaks. He squeaked only once. He took two cuts but he was not long dying' the statement ended.

James Bell, who was in court as a witness against his brother began to argue ownership of the knife but John silenced him by asking. 'Do you mean to say, Jem, that you did not give me your knife to cut the boy's throat? And did you not have part of the money?'

Constable Charles Patterson told the court about the remarks made by John as he was being escorted to Maidstone Gaol, also claiming that John had mentioned the knife and glove in Richard's pocket some time before the body was exhumed.

The final witnesses for the prosecution was draper John Railton, who claimed that John Bell had come into his shop soon after 4 March asking for change for a half crown.

Once Railton had testified, John Bell was asked if he wished to say anything but declined the opportunity to speak. Since no witnesses were called for the defence, it was left to Mr Justice Gaselee to sum up the case for the jury, who took just minutes to find John Any Bird Bell guilty, although they recommended mercy on account of Bell's youth and also what was described as '…the profligate and unnatural manner in which he has been brought up.'

On hearing the verdict, defence counsel Mr Clarkson immediately began arguing that Bell's statement and confession should not have been heard in court. He was quickly overruled by Mr Justice Gaselee, who went on to pass sentence of death, warning Bell that, in spite of the jury's recommendations, he held out not the slightest hope of mercy. Bell heard the verdict as he had conducted himself throughout the whole trial, showing not the slightest flicker of emotion. It was only when the judge ordered that his body should be given to surgeons for dissection that a solitary tear trickled down his cheek.

Bell's execution was scheduled for 1 August 1831 and by 5.00 a.m. almost eight thousand people had already congregated in front of Maidstone Gaol. Inside the prison, John Any Bird Bell continued to conduct himself with the utmost decorum. He wept only when his mother visited him the previous day, accusing her of being the cause of bringing him to what he referred to as his 'present scrape.' After listening to a sermon preached by the prison chaplain, Bell expanded on his confession, admitting that Richard had recognised his murderous intent and had offered to give him all the money he had as well as the knife, if he would spare his life. Richard promised to say nothing to another human being and to love John for the rest of his life if he would release him but John's only response was to thrust the knife into Richard's throat, even as he begged for his life.

At the appointed time, John Any Bird Bell walked firmly to the gallows and waited patiently while the noose was adjusted round his neck. He then repeatedly asked 'Lord have mercy upon us' before addressing the crowd saying 'All the people before me take warning by me.' Asked if he had anything further to say, he continued to intone 'Lord have mercy upon my poor soul' until the executioner's work was done. His body was taken down and handed to surgeons in Rochester for dissection.

Note: There are some discrepancies between contemporary reports of the case. Relieving Officer Mr Cutbath is also named as Cuthbard, while PC Patterson is also named as PC Pattison. James Bell's age is variously given as ten, eleven and twelve years old. Records suggest that he was born in 1819.

'Whosoever sheddeth man's blood, by man shall his blood be shed.'

Church Broughton, Derbyshire, 1835.

By May 1835, thirteen-year-old William Wild had been working as a general servant for farmer Josiah Smith and his family of Church Broughton, Derbyshire, for around a month. It was William's job to fetch the cows for milking, feed the pigs and generally run errands but he was often asked to do jobs in the house as well, including watching Josiah and Ann Smith's three young children. After working at the farm for just two weeks, William was so unhappy that he ran away but was promptly sent back by his mother and stepfather.

On 22 May, Ann Smith's mother, Elizabeth Hall came to visit and found fault with the dirty and disordered state of the house, which she seemed to think was William's job to keep clean. She told William that he was a very indifferent maid and that, if she had such a maid as he, she would knock his head off.

After dinner, Ann instructed William to clean the fire irons, which he did not do. Next she sent him to feed the pigs, complaining later that he hadn't done the job properly. William tried to argue that he had done it the way Mr Smith had taught him but to no avail. Ann then ordered William to go and find her children, who she had earlier seen going off with a neighbour's children. William muttered under his breath that he was 'no maiden' but nevertheless set off to find seven-year-old John, three-year-old Elizabeth and eighteen-month-old Martha.

Thirty minutes later he returned alone and told Ann that she would have to fetch the children herself. They were sitting behind the stile, he explained, and would cry their hearts out if he attempted to bring them home. Ann walked to the stile but couldn't see her children so she continued along the path towards a large pit, from which the cattle drank. As she neared the pit, she was horrified to see Elizabeth floating on the surface.

'Oh, my Bessy, my Bessy' she screamed, peering into the pit to see if she could also see Martha or John. When she could find neither child, she ran as fast as she could towards home, meeting her neighbour Maria Earp on the way. Moments later Ann met William and sent him off to look for her missing children and before long, William shouted back to her that Martha was also in the pit.

Maria Earp's husband William arrived at the pit and with William Wild's assistance, managed to pull the two girls from the water. Although both were quite obviously dead, William Wild was sent the two miles to the nearest village to fetch surgeon, James Adams. It took him over two hours to return with the news that Adams had refused to come but suggested squeezing the little girls and rubbing them well with salt. 'He has not been there at all; my husband had better go' said Maria Earp, and William Earp returned with Adams within half an hour. Although the surgeon could do nothing to revive Elizabeth and Martha, he was able to confirm that he hadn't seen William Wild that day and had received no prior summons to attend to the two drowned children.

An inquest was opened before coroner Mr Henry Mozley on 23 May. However, since there were already strong suspicions that William Wild had had a hand in the deaths of his employer's children, he was taken into custody and detained at the public house where the inquest was due to sit. He was asked about the drownings by several people and gave differing accounts of what happened every time, eventually saying that he had left the two little girls on the banks of the pit while he went off to pick wild flowers for them. When he returned he claimed to have literally tripped over the children, sending them flying into the water. He swore that he had tried to rescue them with a hooked stick.

William's account of the tragedy didn't ring true and eventually two local farmers took it upon themselves to try and establish the truth. In the absence of police constable William Jackson, Mr Wragg took William aside and questioned him how the children got into the pit, asking 'Did they fall in by accident or were they put in?' William refused to answer so, when Wragg left the room, Mr Hopkinson decided to try and get to the bottom of the story.

He invited William to kneel down beside him and asked him to tell the truth in the presence of the Almighty. When Hopkinson repeated Mr Wragg's question, William admitted 'They were put in', although he refused to elaborate further.

William had already made a formal statement to the police and this was read at the inquest:' I can give no other account than I have already given. I was yesterday alone with the two children near the pit; they were about three yards from the edge of the pit when I left them to get some lady smocks. I was two or three minutes away doing this; when I returned back I found that they had got nearer the pit. They had just sat down before I had got the last lady smock. They were sitting together about three quarters of a yard off the edge. As I was returning, Martha being the nearest to me and Bessy was just going to kiss her or clip her, I stumbled against Martha and sent her into the pit first and Bessy immediately after. My left foot did it all. Bessy had hold of Martha behind, with her arm around her waist. I ran up from the side nearest the lane where I had been getting lady smocks up to the side where the tree is and they were sitting together between the lane and the tree. I went sharpish, as hard as I could walk and with me catching my foot, it hurled me on one side but I just caught my left foot. They were facing the pit. I just caught them behind with my foot. They neither of them made any noise in the water but kept sailing on like a fish in the water. I tried to catch hold of their clothes with a hooked stick. There was a bit of hook on it, which soon came off. I don't know how long I was trying to get them, perhaps three or four minutes, when the hook broke, which was very small and then I went home and told the missis they sat against the stile.'

Yet while William's explanation for the deaths was that they had been a tragic accident, the children who had been playing with Bessy and Martha on the day believed otherwise. John Smith and Elizabeth Earp, who were both seven years old, were first questioned about their understanding of the difference between the truth and a lie. Both children were asked if they went to church or chapel, if they knew the Lord's Prayer and if they understood the meaning of an oath. When John and Elizabeth answered all three questions in the affirmative, the coroner asked them separately for their recollections of the afternoon of the drownings.

Both children explained that they were playing in a place called Ox Close, when William came upon them and told them that there were a lot of birds' nests on the opposite side of the hedge. John, Elizabeth and her siblings Abraham and Fanny went off to look, leaving Bessy and Martha with William, who promised that he would give them some 'good stuff' if they went with him.

John and Elizabeth's evidence was corroborated by William Earp and another witness named Elizabeth Fearn, both of whom recalled seeing William alone with the two girls, carrying Martha on his right arm and leading Bessy with his left hand.

The evidence against William Wild led the inquest jury to the conclusion that he was guilty of wilful murder and he was committed to stand trial before Mr Justice Gaselee at the Derbyshire Assizes. When the trial opened on 30 July, William had just passed his fourteenth birthday. Mr Whitehurst and Mr Humfrey handled the case for the prosecution, while, at the request of the judge, Mr Wilmore undertook William's defence.

The witnesses told much the same story as they already had at the inquest. They were joined by Police Constable William Jackson, who told the court that, while conveying William to jail after the inquest, he asked him how he could be so cruel as to leave two children drowning. Admitting that he had made no attempt to get the girls out, William told the constable that he had remained at the side of the pit the whole time they were drowning. 'They were floating about in the water like two blind puppies' he gloated, adding that he was afraid to try and rescue them in case he fell in himself. Jackson asked if someone in the house had done anything to him and the boy claimed that Mrs Smith's mother had scolded him, hit him and called him an idle rascal.

'Thou didst it out of spite?' asked the constable.

'I did' agreed William.

Having repeated the testimony she had given at the inquest, Ann Smith was asked about her dealings with William in the wake of the death of her daughters. 'I asked him how he came to do such a thing and he answered "You should not have come and fetched me again after I ran away"' Ann Smith's reply was that William's mother had made him come back.

'Did you do it for spite?' she asked him.

'Yes, I did.' He replied.

For the defence, Mr Wilmore produced a copy of the statement given by Ann Smith to the coroner, which had no mention of the word 'spite'. He pointed out that, according to her evidence today, William often had charge of the children and that, although he was somewhat awkward and sour looking, she never had any reason to suspect he might feel in the slightest bit malicious towards them. Wilmore also forced an admission from Ann that the pit was such that the children might easily have fallen into it and that, when she first went to find them, that had been her biggest fear.

Once all of the prosecution witnesses had been heard, Mr Justice Gaselee gave William Wild the chance to speak in his own defence. William sobbed but said nothing.

The defence then called their only witness, William's stepfather, Joseph Johnson, who stated that his step-son was of a humane and kind disposition. He stated that William often had charge of his five step-siblings, sometimes for the whole day and had always shown them nothing but kindness. With that the defence rested and it was left to the judge to sum up the evidence for the jury, who retired for only fifteen minutes before returning to pronounce William Wild guilty.

'It was impossible for the jury who have tried you to have arrived at any other conclusion' Gaselee told Wild, adding that he had examined the evidence very carefully to see if it were at all possible to view the case as one of manslaughter. The cause of these children's deaths either came from your hand or that cause was accident. You were either guilty of murder or totally innocent and the jury have rightfully decided. A more cruel and unprovoked murder never came before my observation. The children committed to your care were infants. You made no attempt to rescue them but regarded them, while in the act of drowning, in the most cool and contemptuous manner. In your case, I have no discretion. "Whosoever sheddeth man's blood, by man shall his blood be shed." I entreat of you to make the best use of your remaining time and pray to the Creator to grant you that mercy in another world, which I cannot hold out any hope will be extended to you in this one.' With that, Mr Justice Gaselee sentenced Wild to be hanged, although in view of his youth, the judge ordered the execution to be delayed until the next sitting of the Assizes in November, in order that he might consult with colleagues.

In the event, Wild was not hanged. After a period of detention on the convict ship *Euryalus,* moored at Chatham, on 15 April 1836 he joined two-hundred-and-twenty-nine other convicts on board the ship *Lord Lyndoch* and was transported to Van Diemen's Land. He is believed to have died in Australia.

'Oh, you young rascal, what have you done?'

Lincoln, 1838.

On 7 April, maid servant Susan Quincey was the first person up and about at the Lincoln home of butcher John Bruce. She was joined in the kitchen at around 7.00 a.m. by former butcher's apprentice and now journeyman Thomas Savidge. As Savidge was enjoying his breakfast of bread, boiled milk and cold meat, the butcher's current apprentice, fourteen-year-old Samuel Kirkby came downstairs. He had a wash at the sink and asked Susan to get his breakfast, which he ate before going into the shop. Finally, butcher John Bruce and Mary, one of his daughters, came into the kitchen.

The first thing Bruce did on reaching the kitchen was to clean his teeth and, as he was doing so, he remarked to Mary 'This water tastes very queer.' Bruce then drank two cups of tea, complaining as he did so of a great heat in his throat and stomach.

Within a very short time, people began to feel ill. Susan Quincey vomited, as did Mary Bruce, while John Bruce felt so ill that he sent Kirkby to fetch his doctor. Meanwhile, charwoman Elizabeth 'Betty' Raven arrived to begin her work for the day and soon she too was taken ill.

When surgeon Henry Brooke arrived at the house at around 9.00 a.m., he found John Bruce in his bedroom, exhausted from constant vomiting. Brooke asked Bruce how long he had been ill and the butcher replied that he had felt fine until eating his breakfast. Brooke went back to his surgery to collect some medication for Bruce and Susan Quincey. He was not gone long but, when he returned, he found that Bruce's condition had worsened. His pulse was weak and he was still vomiting uncontrollably and complaining of feeling very thirsty and having an acute burning sensation in his stomach and throat.

Brooke gave Bruce a dose of medicine and the butcher immediately threw it back up. Brooke gave him a different medicine and was then called to the kitchen to examine Betty Raven, who was now showing the same symptoms. Brooke went away for still more medicine and when he returned less than fifteen minutes later, he found John Bruce on the point of death. Between them the surgeon and Mary Bruce managed to get John into bed, where he died almost immediately.

The only two people in the household who had breakfasted but had not been taken ill at that point were Thomas Savidge and Samuel Kirkby and, when Brooke questioned them about what they had eaten for breakfast he discovered that they were the only ones who had not drunk tea. However, when Brooke questioned the char woman, she insisted that she had eaten or drunk nothing since arriving at the house, having taken her breakfast before leaving her home. Then, two women came to the house to help lay out John Bruce and nurse the sick; they too drank tea and, before long, they were displaying the same symptoms as the people they were meant to be caring for.

With Betty Raven's claims apparently ruling out the possibility of poisoning, Brooke began to consider English cholera as the cause of the sickness in the household but the doctor was unable to shake the feeling that the invalids had ingested some sort of noxious substance. He went back to Betty Raven and questioned her again and she admitted that, on arriving she had scraped out the remains of a boiled egg and drained a cup of tea that Mr Bruce had left, adding that she had been hesitant to admit it before, for fear of being dismissed for stealing food.

On hearing this, Brooke took possession of the teapot and kettle and handed them to his partner, surgeon John Hewson, who, with the assistance of surgeon Richard Sutton Harvey, carried out a post-mortem examination on Bruce the day after his death.

On opening Bruce's stomach, Hewson noticed that it was highly inflamed, with many dark, bleeding patches on the stomach wall. There were six or seven places where the mucous membrane had been completely destroyed, leading Hewson to conclude that Bruce had died from the effects of a corrosive poison, such as oxide of arsenic.

On 8 April, coroner James Hitchins opened an inquest at The Spread Eagle Inn, Lincoln, on the death of John Bruce but after hearing from Thomas Savidge and Samuel Kirkby, he adjourned for twenty-four hours to allow doctors to run tests. Hewson then analysed the water remaining in the kettle, which confirmed the presence of arsenic. The coroner took the unusual step of asking Hewson to repeat the tests before the jury and also to demonstrate that testing pure water gave completely different results.

Several people were still too ill to attend the inquest, so the coroner visited them with the foreman of the jury and one other jury member in order to record their depositions. Susan Quincey recalled her master coming down to breakfast and then going into the shop, returning to the kitchen a little later and asking her if she felt all right, having eaten mutton chops for dinner the previous evening. Asked about relationships in the house, Susan claimed that John Bruce and Samuel Kirkby often quarrelled and that Bruce had disciplined his apprentice by confining him to the house on the previous Sunday after he neglected to care for a lamb, which subsequently died. Samuel was allegedly furious, saying that he wished Bruce would drop dead and that he would '…see him out.'

Mary Bruce recalled fetching water for her father to brush his teeth and him complaining that it burned his throat and asking if there were any poison about. Betty Raven now claimed to have been confused when she denied having eaten or drunk anything. She actually drank some tea and scooped some boiled egg from its shell, after which she was taken ill and vomited a great deal.

Having heard the depositions, the coroner then spoke to Rebecca Sparrow, who was called in to lay out John Bruce. Rebecca also drank tea and immediately became unwell, after which Dr Brooke appropriated the kettle and its contents.

Rebecca remembered Samuel Kirkby claiming to have lied when he gave his evidence on the first day of the inquest. Although normally a great lover of tea, it was noted that Samuel took only half a cup when it was offered to him, topping it up with a lot of milk. He also claimed to have been sick overnight but was perfectly well when he got up that morning.

Kirkby was taken into custody and asked police Inspector Thomas Ashton what he was being taken for. Ashton told him that he was suspected of putting poison in the kettle, which had caused the death of Mr Bruce. 'I suppose they'll go to all the druggists in town' Kirkby mused, adding 'if you do, you'll not find anything out.'

Kirkby told Ashton that he too had taken tea that morning and had been sick. He claimed that Bruce frequently thumped him or pulled his ears, but admitted that he usually deserved it. The last occasion had been only a few days before his master's death, when he claimed that Bruce had flown at him like a madman for not tending to a lamb and had prevented him from going out on Sunday as a punishment.

As Kirkby suggested, Ashton visited all of the druggists in the area. Errand boy Joseph Harrison testified that Kirkby had pestered him to obtain some poison for him but that he had refused. Another druggist's errand boy, Joseph Leaf, told much the same story but William Hicks, who was errand boy to chemist and druggist Mr Battle, told the inquest that he had procured some arsenic for Kirkby, who had told him that he wanted to use it to poison rats. Mr Battle's apprentice, William White, testified that Hicks had been asking lots of questions about the arsenic stored in a barrel in the basement of Battle's shop and had been told in no uncertain terms that it was poison and that he was not to go anywhere near it.

Once all of the witnesses had testified, Samuel Kirkby was brought back into the room. He readily admitted that he might have wished John Bruce dead, after his master had severely beaten him but declined to make any other comment.

The inquest jury returned a verdict of wilful murder against Samuel Kirkby, who was sent to Lincoln City Gaol to await his appearance at the Assizes. Before dismissing the inquest, the coroner sent for William Hicks and gave him a severe telling off for his part in procuring the poison with which John Bruce was killed. Fortunately for Hicks, his employer Mr Battle was prepared to stand by him, assuring the coroner that the boy was normally of good character.

Kirkby appeared at the Lincoln Assizes before Mr Justice Bosanquet on 23 July, with Mr Serjeant Adams and Mr Whitehurst prosecuting and Mr Humfrey and Mr Miller acting for the defence. Those witnesses who had been too indisposed to appear at the inquest had now recovered and the first to testify were maid Susan Quincey and Mary Bruce. The latter recalled poison being put down to kill mice about a month before her father died. Susan Quincey was recalled and confirmed that she had put the poison down herself, spreading *Nux vomica* on bread and butter and placing it near the mouse holes.

The Assize Courts, Lincoln (author's collection)

Thomas Savidge recalled getting up at 6.00 a.m. on the morning of Saturday 7 April and going out to tend the sheep, before going into the kitchen for his breakfast. Savidge didn't drink any tea until later that afternoon and told the court that it made him very sick indeed. He also saw Kirkby drinking tea but noticed that, whereas the apprentice usually drank four or five cups at a time, he only drank half a cup, which was mostly milk and then pretended to vomit. Savidge remembered poison being put down to deal with rats in the slaughterhouse and hay barn. He also recalled the poisoned bread and butter being put down but said that it was later picked up and thrown away.

Elizabeth Thompson was one of the women called in on 7 April to help nurse the invalids. She and Rebecca Sparrow both stated that they had drunk tea at the house, which had caused them to vomit.

Both women recalled Samuel Kirkby telling them that he had lied to the coroner at the inquest.

Errand boys Joseph Harrison and Joseph Leaf told the court that, in the days before Bruce's death, Kirkby had tried to persuade them to supply him with poison but they refused. William Hicks then told the court that Kirkby had approached him on 5 April asking for 'white mercury' to poison rats in the slaughterhouse and stable. The next day, Kirkby saw Hicks again and asked him if he had got it. Hicks hadn't but met Kirkby that evening, when he was delivering meat to a boat and gave him about half a tablespoonful of poison, wrapped up in brown paper. Hicks warned Kirkby to keep it out of reach of children and Kirkby reassured him that he knew what he was doing.

On 8 April, Hicks bumped into Kirkby as he was coming out of the stable and commiserated with him on his master's death. Kirkby said nothing, other than to warn Hicks to say nothing to anybody about poison.

The court next heard from the medical witnesses, Drs Brooke, Hewson and Harvey, who had cared for the family and servants when they fell ill and had conducted the post-mortem examination on John Bruce and identified the presence of arsenic in the kettle. They were followed into the witness box by policeman Thomas Ashton, who described apprehending Kirkby and taking him into custody at his police house. Ashton recounted Kirkby's remarks about visiting all of the druggists in the area and stated that this is what he did. When he got to Mr Battle's shop and interviewed Hicks, he discovered that Kirkby had been supplied with poison.

Ashton went back home and confronted Kirkby, saying 'Oh, you young rascal, what have you done?'

Kirkby admitted that William Hicks had given him poison but swore that he had screwed it up in its brown paper wrapper and thrown it into the 'privy'. Ashton took it upon himself to search the waste tank under the toilet at Bruce's premises but found no trace of the paper packet.

It was then left to Mr Humfrey to speak in defence of Samuel Kirkby. He told the court that Samuel was the child of respectable parents and, until now, he had borne an irreproachable character. Humfrey closed by begging the jury to be merciful towards Kirkby, on account of his tender years.

The jury took only twenty minutes to deliberate, returning to pronounce Kirkby guilty of wilful murder. Samuel stood stony-faced as Mr Justice Bosanquet passed the death sentence, his expression betraying not a flicker of emotion.

In the event, Samuel wasn't executed but his sentence was commuted to one of transportation for life and he was moved to the convict ship *Justitia,* which was moored at Woolwich, to await the start of his journey to Australia. In due course, he was put on board the ship *Gilmore,* which left London on 5 October 1838 and arrived at Tasmania on 24 January 1839.

By 1848, Samuel had made an application to marry and, at the age of twenty-five, he married Mary Turnbull. The couple produced six children, although their first child, James Soulby Kirkby died from convulsions at just three days old and another child, William, died aged two from croup. By 1853, Kirkby was described as a licensed victualler. Having first been the licensee for the Bellerive Hotel, from 1853 to 1860, Kirkby was registered as the licensee of The Golden Fleece Hotel both in Kangaroo Point. However, on 22 April 1862, Kirkby died aged forty. The cause of his death was given as 'unsound mind', possibly brought about by excessive drinking.

Note: Thomas Savidge's name is alternatively spelled Savage in some contemporary newspapers. Likewise, the surgeon is named as Brooke, Brookes and Brook in different accounts of the murder.

'Grandfather, some person has attempted to shoot you.'

Hackney, London, 1847

In the autumn of 1847, seventy-four-year-old Samuel Nelme was walking in the garden of his house with his twelve-year-old grandson, William Newton Allnutt, who was slightly behind him. Nelme and the boy were carrying a basket between them, each holding it with one hand, when Nelme heard a noise that sounded like a pistol misfiring. He immediately turned round and William told him 'Grandfather, some person has attempted to shoot you.'

William claimed to have seen a man climbing a tree and escaping over a wall, despite the fact that there was a sixty-foot drop on the other side. An immediate and fruitless search was made for the perpetrator but the following morning a pistol and a bloody handkerchief were discovered lying in the garden and the police were contacted. Their enquiries into the ownership of the pistol led straight to William, who had apparently been seen playing with it only three hours before the incident. However, once they learned of this, William's family closed ranks to hush up the fact that he had apparently attempted to murder his grandfather and no further action was taken. William's mother, Maria Louis Allnutt, recognised the handkerchief as being one of her own and told the police that the blood stains resulted from her having suffered a nosebleed some weeks before. Initially Nelme believed that William had fired the shot at him but was persuaded otherwise by William's mother, who was certain that the incriminating items had been planted as a conspiracy against her son.

Although one of his arms had been amputated after an accident in 1837, Nelme was normally a very healthy, hearty man yet, on 27 October, he complained of feeling unwell and asked for some gruel, which was made for him by his daughter. When maid Maria Buchan went to his room to wake him the following morning she was asked to go for Nelme's doctor, Francis Toulmin. When the doctor arrived, Nelme explained that he was experiencing from 'great pain in the bowels' and had suffered from sickness and diarrhoea overnight. Toulmin believed his patient to be seriously ill and prescribed medicine. When he saw Nelme again at midday, he had already taken two doses and Toulmin suggested that he should drink a little beef tea and some brandy and water. However, by late afternoon, Nelme was dead.

At the request of the coroner Mr Baker, Toulmin and his partner Dr Edward Denis Hacon conducted a post-mortem examination and although there was evidence of severe, potentially fatal heart disease, the doctors found nothing to contradict Toulmin's initial impression that Nelme had died from English cholera. However, as a precaution, Nelme's stomach, intestines and stomach contents were removed and taken to Dr Henry Letheby at the London Hospital for analysis.

On 1 November, Toulmin was contacted by Samuel's wife, Sarah, who had vomited, as had her stepdaughter, William's mother. The doctor took away some leftover arrowroot and powdered sugar that both had eaten. He experimented with the sugar, trying to dissolve it in cold distilled water and, when it would not dissolve, he took it to Dr Letheby, who advised him that, while there was nothing suspicious about the arrowroot, the sugar contained enough arsenic to kill a hundred people. Furthermore, according to the analyst, Nelme's organs and stomach contents also contained arsenic, in sufficient quantities to have proved fatal.

Soon after Nelme's death, the police were called to his home to investigate reports that the old man's gold watch and other items of value were missing. Officers spent more than four hours searching the house and grounds but found no trace of the missing valuables. However, they did find six paper packets of arsenic mixed with oatmeal, breadcrumbs and fragments of cheese which, according to the gardener, had been placed by Nelme to kill rats and mice. Nelme was known to keep arsenic in a locked bureau and, according to Mrs Nelme, the key was missing. However, since she had a duplicate, no effort had been made to find it. The police eventually located it on the floor behind a couch in the back parlour and suspected that it had been hidden there by William.

When William was questioned, he readily admitted to having stolen his grandfather's gold watch, watch chain, seals and eyeglasses and thrown them onto the roof of a neighbouring house. When PC Spinks searched the guttering, he found the items wrapped up in a piece of ticking. William was promptly taken before magistrates and remanded on a charge of stealing the watch, at which he begged forgiveness and admitted to having taken the bureau key and concealed it behind the couch.

At the inquest into Nelme's death, one of the key witnesses was the deceased's wife, who explained that her son-in-law had died in 1845, after which his wife and eight children had come to live with her and Mr Nelme. Mrs Nelme explained that William was a very mischievous but clever boy, with a penchant for reading the newspapers. She theorised that it was possible that he had read accounts of poisonings and was convinced that William alone was responsible for the death of her husband and also the illness that she herself had suffered.

The inquest was adjourned several times but, on the sixth sitting, the jury pronounced that 'Samuel Nelme died from taking sugar with which arsenic had been feloniously mixed by William Newton Allnutt, whom we find guilty of wilful murder.' By that time, William was already in custody in Newgate Prison on a charge of stealing his grandfather's watch and chain and was committed for trial for wilful murder on the coroner's warrant.

The trial opened at the Central Criminal Court, London, on 13 December 1847 and, after hearing the circumstances behind Samuel

Nelme's death, the court heard from William's mother, who explained that her thirty-seven-year-old husband had died two years earlier in a state of complete madness, brought about by drink and epilepsy. Mrs Allnutt told the court that William had suffered two serious head injuries in the past – he had fallen onto a ploughshare and also fallen over on ice. As a consequence he suffered from severe headaches and sometimes claimed to hear voices in his head. He also sleepwalked. Mrs Allnutt related that she had a great deal of trouble with William's morals, stating that whenever he was told off for a misdemeanour, he showed no shame and seemed incapable of appreciating that he had done wrong. In addition, William suffered from both persistent ringworm and scrofula – a form of tuberculosis most common in children.

After hearing this, the judge recalled Dr Letheby to the stand, where he was questioned about William's health. He agreed that sleep walking could be indicative of a disordered state of the brain but added that it could also be produced by an upset stomach or indigestion. Hearing voices could also be a symptom of unsoundness of the brain. However when prison surgeon Mr Gilbert McMurdo was called, he was of the opinion that William was perfectly sane and very capable of knowing the difference between right and wrong. The doctors were also in disagreement about whether or not scrofula was likely to affect the brain.

Dr Edward Henry Payne was a brother-in-law of William's late father and was called to testify to a family history of madness and mental instability. He was of the opinion that William was at least partially insane and that this would prevent him from distinguishing right from wrong. Dr Edward Croucher treated William after one of his falls and gave evidence to state that such an injury might produce epilepsy and mental derangement. Dr Frederick Duesbury had treated William over a period of months for indigestion and scrofula. 'I entertained an opinion that he was very peculiar in the formation of his mind' stated Duesbury, adding that there was '…a peculiarity and eccentricity' about William.

'Do you mean that you consider him permanently insane or liable to occasional derangement' Duesbury was asked.

'My opinion is that it is the early stage of insanity, implicating the moral sentiments, the sense of right and wrong' clarified Duesbury. Asked how this might impact on William's behaviour, Duesbury opined 'I think he would understand that he was poisoning his grandfather, if explained to him, but, at the same time, the sense of right and wrong was not acting with sufficient power to control himself.'

The final opinion on William's sanity was given by Dr John Conolly, physician to the Lunatic Asylum. Having visited William in prison and noted his family history and his symptoms, Conolly felt that the boy was of unsound mind. 'Either his brain is diseased or in an excitable state in which disease is most probably to ensue' he explained, stating that he would very likely become insane in the future.

Two long, rambling and very religious letters that William had written to his mother from prison were read to the court, in which he lamented the consequences of his actions, saying that it made him very miserable to think that he would be cast into hell. 'I feel I am in the depth of sin in its true light' he wrote, begging God for forgiveness and claiming that he had poisoned his grandfather after the old man knocked him over, hurting his head. One of the letters included a full confession, given so that William might go to Heaven. 'If I am transported, I know it will be the death of me, therefore I hope they will pardon me' he concluded.

The jury found William Newton Allnutt guilty of wilful murder but strongly recommended him to mercy on account of his age. Addressing William, presiding judge, Mr Baron Rolfe, stated that, having taken his age into consideration, he was willing to recommend that his life should be spared. However, for the time being, a sentence of death must be recorded and William should understand that, if any remission of the sentence was granted, it would not be from any belief that he was not in a sound state of mind. In the event, should his life be spared, William must expect to pass the whole of the remainder of it in ignominy and disgrace. Hearing this, William became very agitated and had to be supported by one of the turnkeys as he was removed from court.

Newgate Prison, 1905 (author's collection)

William was sent to Newgate Prison, where he spent the next four years before learning that he was to be transported. On 16 July 1851, he boarded the convict sailing ship *Minden,* which arrived in Western Australia on 14 October. Although William went on to earn a ticket of leave, he is reported to have died on 17 April 1853 from phthisis (a form of pulmonary tuberculosis).

Note: In different publications, the date of Nelme's death is given as 22 or 27 October. Mrs Nelme is variously named Suzannah and Sarah, while surgeon Toulmin is also named Doulman.

'Let us throw him into the canal or else we will be catched.'

Liverpool, Lancashire, 1855.

Out-of-work labourer John Fleeson of Liverpool was more than a little preoccupied as he took his regular walk through Stanley Docks in search of work. At lunchtime four days earlier, on 15 July 1855, John's seven-year-old son James had gone out to play with other boys in the neighbourhood of his home in Saltney Street and had never returned. Naturally, his parents, neighbours and the police had been searching high and low for him ever since, but it seemed as if the child had somehow vanished into thin air.

Suddenly, John's attention was attracted to something floating in the quay. PC Robert Melling was on duty at the docks and seeing a man standing on the bridge peering intently at the water, he walked over to see what he was looking at. 'That is the body of my son, who has been lost since Sunday' John told the policeman as he approached.

Melling arranged to have the body removed from the water and surgeon George Kemp later carried out a post-mortem examination. Although Kemp found that the cause of James's death was drowning, he also observed a wound over the boy's right eye, which seemed to have been caused by something hard and rough. The doctor was convinced that this wound occurred before James's death. In addition, Kemp noted that the membranes of the external surface of James's brain were more than usually congested, although he was unable to state with any degree of certainty whether this was due to violence or to suffocation from drowning.

The police questioned some of the boys who had been out playing with James and learned that a quarrel had arisen between him and a boy named Alfred Fitz, which culminated in Fitz hitting James on the head with a brick. James instantly fell to the ground and, after watching him writhing in agony for a while, nine-year-old

Fitz enlisted the help of another boy, eight-year-old John Breen, to throw James into the canal.

Inspector Thomson went to arrest Alfred, who lived in the same street as his alleged victim. As he attempted to take the boy into custody, Alfred's father became violent and threatened to stab the inspector. John Breen proved easier to arrest. Liverpool was the first city in England to set up what were known as 'night asylums' – hostels for the homeless. Breen's mother had taken her family to the night asylum, prior to arranging a passage to Ireland for herself and her three children.

Both Alfred and John were present at the inquest. On the first day, both boys were tearful but by the second and final day of the proceedings, they had become somewhat blasé and hardly seemed aware of the seriousness of their position. Both were barefoot, described by the contemporary newspapers as appearing to be '…in a state of great neglect.'

Along with John Fleeson, PC Melling and surgeon Kemp, the inquest heard from several of the boys who had been playing on the street that day, among them nine-year-old John Hawkins, the son of a tailor from Brunswick Place, Saltney Street. Hawkins described playing leapfrog with a group of children, including James Fleeson, Alfred Fitz and John Breen.

According to Hawkins, Alfred fell out with James, accusing him of not jumping properly. The quarrel between them rumbled on for half an hour or so, before Alfred picked up a half brick and hit James with it on his right temple. James fell to the ground and Alfred hit him again.

James, who was bleeding heavily, never spoke but lay on the ground whimpering, thrashing his arms and legs convulsively. Eventually, Alfred took him by the arms and John Breen by the legs and between them they dragged James around forty yards to the canal and threw him in, before running away. James struggled for a couple of minutes before sinking beneath the surface of the water. Hawkins, who was only one of a number of boys who witnessed the attack on James, claimed that he told his parents what had happened that night and that his parents had then tried to find James's father but had not succeeded.

A woman named Mary Ann Spratt told the inquest that she had seen Fitz striking a little boy on the afternoon of 15 July, although she could not say for certain that the child being struck was James Fleeson. Mrs Spratt remonstrated with Fitz, who told her to mind her own business, before hitting the child again and knocking him down. Mrs Spratt claimed that Fitz then kicked the child as he lay on the ground, stating that a man had then separated the two boys. However when James Hawkins was recalled before the coroner, he could remember neither Mrs Spratt nor a man intervening in the fight.

Having summed up the case for the jury, the coroner asked them what they thought had caused James Fleeson's death. After a short discussion, the jury advised the coroner that they believed that the deceased was drowned. The coroner then asked them to consider the circumstances under which the boy was drowned. 'It is an extraordinary case' he commented, pointing out that the victim killed was a child, the chief witness was a child and the two prisoners were both children. The coroner had no doubt that the jury would be asking themselves 'Can these children be guilty of the crime of murder?'

The law stated that no infant under the age of seven years old could be punished for a criminal act but, between the ages of seven and fourteen, a child was deemed capable of committing a crime. If the jury were of the opinion that two such children as these before them were not guilty of murder they must discharge them. If they believed the children were guilty, in three weeks' time, the boys would be taken to the Assizes to be tried on that charge.

After a short deliberation, the jury told the coroner that, while they were unanimously agreed that the boys had committed murder, they were reluctant to send two such young boys for trial at the Assizes. The coroner reassured them that under no circumstances would Fitz and Breen be put to death. On the contrary, they might be placed under better care than they had been and it might be the means of making them realise the awfulness of the crime with which they were charged.

When the inquest jury returned a verdict of wilful murder against Alfred Fitz and John Breen, both boys began to sob. Breen pleaded that he knew nothing about it and accused James Hawkins of telling lies. Fitz also insisted that he had never struck James Fleeson but the boys' protests were in vain.

Their trial took place at the Lancashire Assizes, before Mr Baron Platt. Mr Brett prosecuted the case and, while Mr Aspinall had been appointed to defend Fitz, no counsel had been arranged for Breen. At the request of the judge, Mr Cross agreed to undertake Breen's defence.

Counsel for the prosecution opened by explaining the law regarding the culpability of children. Since Fitz and Breen were older than seven but younger than fourteen years old, in order to prove the crime of murder against them, it was necessary not only to show that they committed an act, the natural consequences of which would be and was the death of another person, but also to prove that they knew at the time that this would cause death.

Brett then outlined the facts of the case for the jury, describing the argument that arose between the deceased and Fitz over a game of leapfrog. Having struck James twice on the head with a brick, Fitz told Breen 'Let us throw him into the canal or else we will be catched.'

'Yes, I will help you' Breen replied and between them they carried James for forty yards and threw him into the canal, which eventually emptied into the quay at Stanley Docks, where the boy's body was found.

Brett told the jury that, if these facts were proved and they were satisfied that the prisoners intended that the child should die and that his death should be concealed, it would be their duty to find them guilty of this serious charge, regardless of their tender age. However, if the jury believed that the boys had injured Fleeson without intent and, supposing him dead, had then thrown him into the canal as an attempt to conceal his body; this would amount to manslaughter rather than murder.

As at the inquest, the main witnesses were PC Melling, surgeon Kemp, John Hawkins and Mary Ann Spratt. Once again, Hawkins's evidence contradicted that of Mrs Spratt, since he could not recall seeing her and did not hear Fitz telling anyone to mind her own business. Fitz's defence counsel tried to discredit Mrs Spratt, informing the court that she once lodged with Mrs Fitz and suggesting that she was turned out of the house for stealing a sovereign. Mrs Spratt vigorously denied this, assuring the court that she left of her own accord because the lodgings didn't suit her.

After only a brief deliberation, the jury found both boys guilty of manslaughter, accompanying their verdict with a strong recommendation to mercy. Mr Baron Platt summoned Mr Gibbs, the then governor of Liverpool Borough Gaol. 'If these boys are sent to the house of correction, how would they be treated?' asked the judge.

'They would be instructed by the schoolmaster, under the direction of the chaplain, and kept in partial separate confinement' replied Gibbs.

'They would be taught to read and write?'

'They would, my Lord.'

'I find they can do neither.'

'There has been an attempt to teach them since they have been in gaol.' Gibbs responded.

'I will send them to you, so that they may be instructed' Mr Baron Platt decided. 'They will not be put to any labour, I suppose?'

'Very little and very light labour only, my Lord.'

Mr Baron Platt turned his attention to Fitz and Breen. 'You did not mean to kill this little boy, certainly, when you put him into the water but I will see if I can make you keep out of more mischief by having you a little instructed before you get out of prison again. The greatest mercy I can show you is to send you to prison for twelve months. You will have a schoolmaster and a chaplain to instruct you and you will be taught how to get your own living.' With that, the boys were taken from court to begin their sentence.

Note: Some contemporary reports of the case name Alfred Fitz as Alfred Fitzpatrick. John Hawkins is also named James Hawkins in some publications, while Mary Ann Spratt is also named as Mary Ann Pratt.

'What are you doing with that child undressed?'

Stockport, Cheshire, 1861.

Two-year-old George Thomas Burgess of Stockport, Cheshire, had two younger brothers and, since both of his parents worked full time as cotton weavers, George was placed with a nurse, who cared for him day and night at her home.

On 11 April 1861, George's nurse Sarah Ann Warren got the toddler up at around seven o'clock, dressing him in the fashion of the day in a red flannel waistcoat, calico shirt, petticoat, brown skirt, plaid skirt and a plaid over frock. By two o'clock that afternoon, George and another child were playing with a wheelbarrow on a piece of waste land opposite his nurse's house in Shawcross Street. However, when Sarah went to check on her charge half an hour later, little George was nowhere to be seen.

Sarah began a frantic search for the toddler, asking her neighbours if they had seen him and, when she was unable to locate him, she went to the police to report him missing. When George's father Ralph visited the nurse on his way home from work that evening and learned that his boy was lost, he employed the town crier to broadcast the news and spent all night walking the streets and searching the nearby fields for his son.

Just after noon on 12 April, labourer John Buckley was working in Ford's Field, near the brook in Love Lane, Stockport when, out of the corner of his eye, he saw something pink in the water. A closer investigation revealed the body of a toddler, naked apart from a pair of clogs. Since the child was lying face down, it was obviously dead, so Buckley didn't disturb it but sent for the police. When Inspector William Walker arrived on the scene, he noted that only the child's buttocks and back of the head protruded from the shallow water. The child's back and legs were covered in welts, as if they had been lashed.

Walker retrieved the body from where it lay, face pressed on a stone on the bed of the stream. The dead child was a little boy, whose clothes were found a few yards away on the bank of the stream. A single stocking was found further upstream, all of the clothes being completely dry. The policeman was certain that the toddler's death was no accident, since the water was shallow and the banks little more than a gentle incline – had the child fallen into the stream accidentally, he should have been able to extricate himself without difficulty. Furthermore, Walker noticed footmarks in the mud at the side of the stream. Some matched the clogs still worn by the little boy, but there were also larger footmarks, which suggested the presence of at least two other people.

The dead child was taken to the nearby White Horse Tavern to await the attention of the coroner, while police began their enquiries by talking to those people who lived near to Love Lane. They soon found three people who had seen a young child on 11 April, in the company of two older boys.

Shortly before three o'clock, Mary Whitehead saw two boys dragging along a toddler, who was crying and seemed unwilling to go with them. Mary asked the boys where they were going and was told 'Down Love Lane.'

An hour later, Emma Williams and her thirteen-year-old son saw the threesome. By this time, the toddler was naked and, as Emma and her son watched, the smaller of his two companions grabbed a twig out of the hedgerow and whipped the toddler across the back of his legs.

'What are you doing with that child undressed?' Emma called to the boys, who did not reply but immediately ran off towards Love Lane. Emma and Frank Williams and Mary Whitehead all gave very similar descriptions of the two boys, telling the police that one was rather stout and wore dark clothes and a cap, while the other was slighter in build and wore a loose tunic.

Meanwhile, news reached Ralph Burgess that a little boy had been found dead and he and Sarah Warren went to The White Horse, where they identified the body as being that of George Burgess. A post-mortem examination conducted by surgeon Thomas Massey revealed numerous lash wounds to the child's back and buttocks, along with injuries to his head, apparently caused by him being hit with a stick. According to Massey, all of the injuries were produced while the little boy was alive but, while the blows to his head may well have stunned him, the cause of death was 'suffocation from drowning', after the little boy's face had been pressed down onto the bed of the stream and held there.

An inquest on George's death was opened by coroner William Johnson on 13 April. After hearing evidence of identity from Ralph Burgess, the coroner called Sarah Ann Warren to detail the circumstances of her charge's disappearance. Having described the clothes that George was wearing on the day of his death, Sarah was questioned as to whether or not she thought it would have been possible for George to undress himself. Sarah explained that the child's waistcoat was tied at the front, whereas his two skirts were buttoned at the back and the overdress he wore was fastened with hooks and eyes. Because of the complexity of his garments, Sarah was adamant that someone else had to have undressed him. After hearing from the man who found the body, surgeon Massey, Inspector Walker and the three witnesses who had seen George with two older boys, the coroner adjourned the inquest to allow the police more time to conduct their enquiries.

After conducting numerous interviews, the police believed that they had identified the two boys seen with the toddler as Peter Henry Barratt and James Bradley, both of whom were eight years old. They first went to visit Barratt at his home in Middle Hillgate, where they found the boy's father cutting a man's hair. Told that the police wished to speak to his son in connection with the murder of George Burgess, Peter Barratt told PC William Morley that he thought it was highly unlikely that the boy was involved. 'He's in the kitchen. See what he says about it' Barratt told the policeman.

After a few words with Peter Henry Barratt, with his father's permission, Morley asked the boy to accompany him to Bradley's house. While Peter Barratt had seemed disinterested in what the police had to say to his son, John Bradley insisted on being present while his son was interviewed.

After asking both boys about school, P.C. Morley asked Peter who he had played with on 11 April.

'With Jemmy [James] Bradley' replied Peter.

'Where did you go?'

'We went beside the Star Inn'

'Which way did you go then?' asked the policeman.

'Down the narrow lane by the Star Inn, down Hampshaw Lane and up Love Lane'.

'Was there anyone else with you?' probed Morley.

James replied 'A little boy we met beside the Star Inn.'

'Did you see anyone in Love Lane?'

'Yes, we saw a woman' James continued.

'Where did you go afterwards?'

'We went down Love Lane until we got to a hole with some water in it.'

'What did you do then?'

'Peter said I must undress it.'

'Thou undressed it as well as me.' Peter interjected.

'So you both undressed it?'

'Yes' replied James.

'What did you do then?'

'Peter pushed it in the water and I took my clogs off and went in and took it out again and Peter said it must have another.'

'Another what?' Morley asked.

'Another dip in the water' explained James. 'Peter then got a stick out of the hedge and hit it.'

'Thou hit it as well as me' Peter protested.

The boys went on to tell the police constable that they had hit the little boy on his back and on his head '…until it was dead'

'Was it quite dead when you left it?'

'Yes'

'Did you leave it in the water?'

'Yes' replied James.

Having secured both boys in the town lock-up, Morley took their footwear, finding that they compared exactly to the footmarks left on the side of the brook.

When the inquest resumed on 16 April, both boys were brought before the coroner. Mary Whitehead was positive that Bradley and Barratt were the two boys she had seen with George shortly before his death, telling the inquest that James was the boy who had hold of the toddler's arm and was dragging him along. Emma Williams was less certain of her identification. She was certain that Bradley was one of the boys, agreeing that he was holding George's hand when she spoke to them. However, she was less sure about the identity of Barratt.

It was revealed that Barratt was wearing different clothes that day and P.C. Morley was despatched to the boy's home to collect the tunic he was wearing on 11 April. As soon as she saw it, Emma began to cry and both she and her son were able to positively identify Barratt as the second boy.

With that, the coroner began summing up the case for the jury. There was no doubt that the immediate cause of George's death was suffocation from drowning but there was absolutely nothing to suggest that his death had been accidental. Although the two boys before them today had no motive for their horrifyingly brutal attack on the defenceless toddler, they had chosen a secluded place to do it and had given unquestionable proof of what the coroner described as '…their consciousness of guilt.'

The law stated that, before the age of seven, children could not be found guilty of - or be punished for - a capital offence. However, between the ages of eight and fourteen, it was presumed that a child was capable of differentiating between good and evil. If they believed that the child's death was caused by these two boys, the jury must satisfy themselves that the boys were, at the time, capable of knowing right from wrong. If this was their belief, then the only possible verdict for the jury to return was one of wilful murder.

The jury immediately returned a verdict of wilful murder against Peter Henry Barratt and James Bradley, who were committed under the coroner's warrant to stand trial at Chester Assizes. They were taken to Chester Castle to await the commencement of the proceedings.

Their trial took place on 8 August before Mr Justice Crompton, with Mr Swetenham and Mr Wood prosecuting, while Mr Morgan Lloyd acted in defence of both boys. Lloyd referred to Barratt and Bradley as '...mere babies themselves, who could not have known the crime they committed.' Mr Justice Crompton appeared to agree, remarking in his summary for the jury that it seemed '...straining the case to charge such young children with the crime of wilful murder.' Crompton told the jury that the key to their deliberations was establishing whether or not they believed that the defendants knew right from wrong. If not, then the presumption of malice made by the law would be rebutted, thus reducing the crime from murder to manslaughter.

Chester Castle: Site of the Assizes and also the prison (author's collection)

Having been given the chance of a softer option, the jury were quick to pronounce both boys guilty of the lesser offence of manslaughter, to the obvious approval of the judge, who informed the court that he intended to send the boys to the Bradwall Reformatory School in Cheshire. It was to be hoped, continued Crompton, that by removing the boys from their unsuitable companions in Stockport and teaching them better things they might become better boys.

Bradley and Barratt had been laughing and joking while the jury deliberated their fate. Now both began to cry as Crompton leaned down from his elevated seat to address them. 'I am afraid you have been very wicked, naughty boys and I have no doubt that you have caused the death of this little boy by the brutal way in which you used him. I am going to send you to a place where you will have an opportunity of becoming good boys, for you will have a chance of being brought up in a way you should be and I doubt not but that in time, when you come to understand the nature of the crime, you will repent what you have done.' With that, Crompton sentenced the boys to one month's imprisonment with hard labour, followed by five years at the Reformatory.

Bradley was indeed sent to Bradwall, to be released on licence on 28 January 1866, after which it has proved impossible to track his whereabouts. Records suggest that Barratt was sent to an institution in Warwickshire. It is thought that he eventually married and sired several children, before immigrating to Canada in later life, where he subsequently died.

Note: The labourer who found George's body is alternatively named John Butler in some publications. Some accounts state that, with the exception of one stocking on the bank, all of George's clothes were found in the stream. Although it has no real bearing on the case, it is interesting to note that the post-mortem examination on little George Burgess found that, in his too-short life, he had already twice suffered a broken arm and had been both burned and severely scalded.

'I saw you do it and run away, Jack.'

Birmingham, 1874

Fourteen-year-old Patrick Dunlavey worked as an iron polisher at a factory. His fifteen-year-old neighbour, John Thomas Kirkham, worked at the same place and the boys normally walked home to Milk Street, Birmingham together.

After finishing work on 2 February 1874, they were walking along Cheapside when they met up with a gang of twenty or thirty boys hanging around at the end of an alleyway leading to Bradford Street. As they passed the group, a youth known by the nickname 'Prinny Mack' called out to Kirkham 'Why don't you try to square this slog with me?'

Kirkham was the leader of a group of boys known as the Milk Street Lot, who were at war with a rival gang, the Park Street Set. The two gangs frequently engaged in 'slogging' – pitched battles fought with stones, knives, belt buckles or any other missile that came to hand. However, on that particular night, Kirkham didn't seem in the mood for fighting. 'I haven't anything to do with the slog' he replied.

With that, the leader of the Park Street Set, John 'Jacky' Joyce, suddenly ran out of the crowd and lunged at Dunlavey, who stepped aside to avoid the blow. Joyce then seized Kirkham's neck with his left hand and, with his right, plunged a knife into Kirkham, before running away, leaving the blade buried to the hilt in his rival's neck.

Shoemaker William Thomas heard shouts of 'murder' and saw a youth staggering about in the road as if drunk. Spotting the knife, Thomas grabbed it and pulled it out and was immediately drenched by blood pulsing from the wound. Together with other witnesses, Thomas helped Kirkham to walk to a nearby chemist's shop, where the proprietor summoned a cab to take the badly injured youth to Queen's Hospital.

He was examined by house surgeon Gilbert Smith, who found a three-quarter-inch stab wound, located about two inches below and behind Kirkham's right ear. The direction of the wound suggested that the knife had been forcefully thrust into the boy's neck from behind, travelling in a forward and downward direction.

Kirkham was admitted into hospital, where he remained until his eventual death on 28 February. A post-mortem examination gave the cause of his death as exhaustion, consequent to blood loss from a perforated vertebral artery. While hospitalised, Kirkham gave a deposition to PC Shepherd, in which he accused Jacky Joyce of having stabbed him. Joyce was later brought to Kirkham's bedside and was positively identified by his victim, who told him 'I saw you do it and run away, Jack'.

Joyce, who was described in the contemporary newspapers as 'a sharp, healthy-looking boy', was present at an inquest held by the Birmingham borough coroner Dr Birt Davies and struggled to take the proceedings seriously, at one stage being almost overcome by a fit of giggles and stuffing his cap into his mouth to stifle his laughter.

After hearing evidence of identification from Kirkham's mother Eliza, the coroner heard from several people who had witnessed either the stabbing or its immediate aftermath. Among them was Patrick Dunlavey, who stated that although he was only about eighteen inches away from Kirkham at the time, it was too dark for him to see who had actually stabbed him. Pressed by the coroner, Dunlavey admitted that he believed that he had recognised Joyce from his clothes.

Thirteen-year-old Thomas Sheridan told the inquest that, shortly before he was stabbed, Kirkham had asked him if there were any Park Street lads present on Cheapside and from this Sheridan assumed that Kirkham was looking for a 'slog'. Although there was no fight between the two rival gangs that evening, Sheridan claimed to have clearly seen Jacky Joyce stabbing Kirkham in the neck before running away.

William Thomas then recalled helping Kirkham to the pharmacy, from where he was transported to hospital.

Surgeon Gilbert Smith told the inquest about Kirkham's admission to and subsequent stay in hospital and also described his findings at the post mortem examination. Finally, PC Shepherd produced the deposition made by Kirkham, in the belief that he was on his death bed, in which he directly accused Joyce of stabbing him.

In his summing up, the coroner condemned the practice of using a knife in fights. He reminded the inquest jury that the evidence against Joyce was clear, adding that the crime had not been committed in the heat of the moment but was a deliberate and malicious attack by one youth on another, which could justify no other verdict than one of wilful murder. The jury took only a few minutes to deliberate, before returning that very verdict and Joyce was committed to stand trial on the coroner's warrant.

The trial took place at the Warwickshire Assizes on 6 July 1874. Standing before Mr Justice Denman, Joyce still seemed unconcerned, stating quite firmly when asked that he didn't do it.

Mr A. H. Adams Q.C. opened the case for the prosecution, conceding that he did not believe that there was any direct malice expressed against Kirkham by the accused. Nevertheless, Adams maintained that Joyce was guilty as charged, although he added that if the defence could produce any extenuating circumstances he would not argue too strenuously against them.

After the court had heard from those witnesses who appeared at the inquest, Mr Buzzard began his defence of Joyce. He reminded the jury that there was no fighting between the gangs that night and the Park Street boys were not out looking for a quarrel. Indeed, based on Thomas Sheridan's evidence, Buzzard contended that it was Kirkham who was looking for 'bother' – was he really the innocent victim that the prosecution had portrayed?

Buzzard cross-examined surgeon Gilbert Smith, who was forced to concede that Kirkham's injury could have resulted from a knife being thrown at him and embedding itself in his neck. It was a very dark night, argued Buzzard, who reminded the jury that whereas Sheridan had positively identified Joyce as having stabbed Kirkham, Dunlavey, who was only eighteen inches away, had insisted that it was too dark for him to properly recognise the person who had stabbed his neighbour.

According to Buzzard, the accused was a mere child, who had no motive to kill Kirkham and who had insisted all along that the large pocket knife used did not belong to him. William Thomas had stated in court that, as Kirkham staggered around bleeding, there had been boys fleeing in all directions. Buzzard told the jury that the most likely explanation for Kirkham's death was a fight between the two gangs, during which a knife had been thrown by an unidentified assailant.

Mr Justice Denman (author's collection)

In his summary of the evidence, Mr Justice Denman first began by addressing the matter of Joyce's age. In the court calendar, it was stated that the accused was only thirteen years old, which was the age he had given when he was first taken into custody. Yet the police were absolutely sure that Joyce was fourteen years old and his age had significant bearing on the possible verdict.

If he were between the ages of seven and fourteen, Joyce could only be held responsible for his crime if the jury were of the opinion that it was done with malice and the intention to take away a life.

However, if he was fourteen years or older, there need be no evidence of malice to constitute the crime of wilful murder, since the law assumed that malice was present.

After summarising the evidence, Denman told the jury that they must decide whether they believed that Joyce was thirteen or fourteen years old. If they believed he was thirteen, they must satisfy themselves that there was a personal malice against Kirkham and that, in doing what he did, Joyce intended to kill him. In the absence of such evidence, they might find Joyce guilty of the lesser offence of manslaughter.

The jury deliberated for five minutes, before returning to find Joyce guilty of manslaughter, recommending mercy on account of his age. Mr Justice Denman announced his intention to defer sentencing, so it wasn't until the next day that John Joyce learned that he was to serve one month in prison, followed by five years in a reformatory, where Denman advised him to spend his time wisely, '…not quarrelling with his fellows but in self-improvement'. Sadly, the judge's advice fell on deaf ears since no sooner had Joyce left the reformatory than he was up in court again, this time for having attacked two men with a belt. He was sentenced to four months imprisonment with hard labour.

Note: Witness Patrick Dunlavey is alternatively named Dunlaney in some publications.

'Now I have told you the solid truth.'

Fishtoft, Lincolnshire, 1875 / 1876.

On the afternoon of 19 February 1876, nine-year-old William Henry Heblewhite of Fishtoft in Lincolnshire was sent to his grandmother's house with a basket of clean washing. He delivered the freshly laundered clothes and stayed at his grandmother's house chatting for about half an hour, before setting off at dusk to walk home, carrying the basket that now contained dirty linen. He was seen walking towards Fishtoft church at around 5.40p.m. Then around five minutes later he was spotted a little closer to the church, now accompanied by another boy, eleven-year-old William Gilbert Harrod.

Meanwhile, at Heblewhite's home, William's father was waiting for him to get back so that they could to go to Boston Market. As the evening progressed with no sign of the boy, Frederick Overton Heblewhite sent another of his sons to try and find him but Frederick junior returned with the news that his brother had left their grandmother's house some time earlier and should have been home a long time ago. Mr Heblewhite eventually went to the market without William, returning via The Red Cow public house to ask if anyone had seen his son. Many of the villagers offered to help him to search through the night for the missing boy.

The Red Cow Inn, Fishtoft (author's collection)

At around 9.00 a.m. on 20 February, shepherd James Griffin was on his way to tend his flock when he spotted a basket lying close to a deep pit, in a field near the church known as Church Ground. After feeding his sheep, Griffin went for a closer look and was alarmed to see blood on the basket and on the ground around it. Knowing that William was missing, Griffin went straight to the boy's father's house and Heblewhite, Simpson and a third man raced back to the pit with poles and rakes.

The pit was evidently the scene of foul play. In the mud near the water's edge were the impressions of two pairs of children's feet, one set slightly bigger than the other. Griffin could also see the distinct pattern of corduroy at the very edge of the pit, as if someone wearing corduroy trousers had knelt there. A boy's cap lay on the grass and there were three stack pins – wooden stakes used to secure haystacks – two floating on the water and a third lying in a thorn fence at the water's edge.

The three men dragged the water for almost an hour, before finally snagging William Heblewhite's body and pulling it to the pit bank, where it was later stripped and examined by Dr J. E. Tuxford. The doctor noted that William's fingers were clenched around handfuls of mud. There was a cut across the bridge of the boy's nose and right eye, which was very swollen. William's nose was broken and he had a two-inch-long cut on top of his head and severe bruising above his left eyebrow. Tuxford believed that the wounds might have stunned William or perhaps even rendered him unconscious but were unlikely to have proved fatal. At a more detailed post-mortem examination, the doctor found severe bruising on William's scalp at the top of his head. The boy's lungs were black and full of froth and water, leading Tuxford to the conclusion that the cause of death was drowning.

On finding out that William Heblewhite had last been seen in the company of William Harrod, the police went straight to the Harrod's house, where Inspector Thorsby asked him if he had seen Heblewhite yesterday. Harrod admitted that he had seen the boy walking across the common at around 6.00 p.m. but told the inspector that he hadn't spoken to him. Thorsby asked Harrod when he came home, to which the boy replied that it was a little after 6.00 p.m.

Thorsby asked to see the clothes Harrod had been wearing and accompanied him upstairs, where he produced a pair of trousers, a vest and a jacket, which had been hanging on the foot of the bed. Thorsby took the garments downstairs to examine them in better light. Finding bloodstains on the trousers, he asked Harrod if he could account for them. 'I know you cut your finger last week', Harrod's mother Eliza interjected.

The Inspector asked if he could examine Harrod's finger but could see no evidence of any recent wounds. 'It's better now' Harrod explained.

Thorsby charged Harrod with murdering William Henry Heblewhite on the previous day. 'I did not do it' the boy protested, as he was taken away to be detained in the lock up at Boston's Skirbeck Quarter.

The police seized a pair of Harrod's boots, which were compared to the impressions found on the pit bank and the irregular pattern of nails in the heels proved an exact match. Thorsby sent Harrod's trousers, waistcoat, jacket, woollen shirt and neck tie to county analyst Dr Lowe, along with the three stack pins, the basket and some turf from the pit bank. Lowe found common duck weed, consistent with that from the pit, in the hem at the bottom of the trouser legs. The blood extracted from the garments was shown to be human in origin, as was that on the turf and basket. Lowe also found a single light brown human hair adhering to the front of Harrod's trousers, which was identical to William Heblewhite's hair.

All of this evidence against Harrod was detailed in an inquest held at The Red Cow Inn, presided over by coroner Walter Clegg. However, perhaps the most damning piece of evidence was a letter written by Harrod to his mother from his prison cell, in which he made a full confession. 'Now I have told you the solid truth' he wrote, claiming that, having met up with William Heblewhite, William asked him to go and look at some lambs. According to Harrod, the younger, smaller boy then challenged him to a fight and, when Harrod refused, William picked up a stake and hit him hard on the legs with it twice. Angered, Harrod took another stake and hit William four times on the head and twice on the face. This made William swear at him, so Harrod shoved him into the pit and, after watching him floundering about in the water for a while, he ran home leaving William to his fate.

When this letter was produced, the foreman of the jury asked for the village schoolmaster to be sent for to identify Harrod's handwriting. Mr Soar was duly summoned and positively identified the script, adding that he was certain that it had been written by Harrod, who had a unique way of forming the letter F.

It was almost a foregone conclusion that the inquest jury would return a verdict of wilful murder against William Harrod, who was committed for trial at the next Lincolnshire Assizes on the coroner's warrant. Yet in the wake of the inquest, even more shocking information emerged.

On 2 October 1875, a five-year-old Fishtoft boy named Arthur Hockley was found drowned in a pit close to his home. Coroner Dr Clegg held an inquest but could find nothing to suggest how the child came to be in the water, so an open verdict was returned. After the inquest on William Heblewhite, it was remembered that William Harrod had been the last person seen with Hockley; indeed, he had given evidence at the inquest into Hockley's death and had been given a shilling by the coroner for doing so.

Further enquiries were made and it was discovered that Harrod had actually admitted to three boys that he had pushed Hockley into the water and left him to drown. When the statement Harrod had made to the coroner at Hockley's inquest was demonstrated to be untruthful, Harrod was further charged with a second count of wilful murder.

By the time of his trial before Mr Justice Lindley at the Lincolnshire Assizes, William Gilbert Harrod had celebrated his twelfth birthday. After hearing all the evidence relating to the death of William Heblewhite, the judge decided that there was no point in proceeding with the charge of the wilful murder of Arthur Hockley. The jury found Harrod guilty of manslaughter and, in view of his age, Mr Justice Lindley sentenced him relatively lightly to fifteen years' penal servitude. Records suggest that Harrod spent much of his sentence in Dartmoor Prison and that he eventually died there aged twenty-one in 1884.

Note: Victim William Heblewhite is alternatively named Hebblewhite and Ablewhite in contemporary accounts of the murder. Likewise, Arthur Hockley is sometimes named as Stockley.

'I did not intend to kill the man.'

Everton Brow, Liverpool, Lancashire, 1886

The work day was coming to an end at Barton's Timber Yard in Byron Street, Liverpool, when sixteen-year-old Michael Lavelle turned up and began to mooch around. He spoke to seventeen-year-old William Roberts, asking him how he was getting on and how long he had been working at the yard, commenting that he was supposed to have started work there too. He then wandered over to a boiler and began messing about with it. Sawyer Maxwell Kirkpatrick told him to leave it alone. Lavelle immediately did as he was asked, walking over to Kirkpatrick and speaking to him for a couple of minutes.

When the men finished work, Lavelle was still hanging around and asked Roberts which way he was going home and whether or not he normally walked home with Kirkpatrick. Roberts told him that, since he had to pass Kirkpatrick's door, they usually walked together.

At this, Lavelle bid Roberts goodnight and left. Roberts and Kirkpatrick set along Richmond Row. They had reached the Congregational Chapel in Everton Crescent when Lavelle suddenly appeared behind them and shouted 'Hello Mac.' Roberts turned round, just in time to see Lavelle swinging a heavy wooden roller, which he was holding in both hands. The roller hit Kirkpatrick behind his right ear, knocking him to the ground.

Lavelle ran away, leaving William Roberts to tend to Kirkpatrick, who lay unconscious on the pavement. After about five minutes, he slowly regained his senses and Roberts managed to haul him to his feet and prop him up against some railings. 'What hit me?' he asked dazedly.

Leaning on Roberts, Kirkpatrick managed to stagger home, where his wife Jane was waiting for him. He asked her if there was any blood on his head and she told him that there wasn't, although there was some in his ear and on his neck. At her insistence, Kirkpatrick went to see his doctor and Dr Ellis told him to go home and go straight to bed, promising to visit him later that night. Ellis did indeed visit at 9.00 p.m., advising bed rest but soon afterwards, forty-two-year-old Kirkpatrick lapsed into unconsciousness and by 10.00 a.m. the next morning, he was dead. When Ellis carried out a post-mortem examination, he determined the cause of death to be compression of the brain, due to bleeding, as a result of a fractured skull.

Naturally, on the assault on Kirkpatrick being reported to them, the police went straight to Lavelle's home in Addison Street, where they found him in bed. Ordered to get up and get dressed, he asked Detective Sergeant Macdonald and Sub-Inspector Hale 'What for?'

'For seriously assaulting Mr Kirkpatrick in Everton Brow last night' replied Macdonald

Lavelle immediately began to cry. 'I used to work with him at Tickle's Timber Yard and he was always getting on at me. He told me that my mother was in hell and I had it in for him after that. I struck him on the top of the head with a stick. I then went along Whatmough Street and dropped the stick.' When the police were made aware of Kirkpatrick's death, Lavelle was charged with his wilful murder. 'I know I did the deed. I want some witnesses' he sobbed.

An inquest on the death of Maxwell Kirkpatrick was presided over by coroner Mr Clarke Aspinall. The chief witness was William Roberts, but a former employee at Tickle's also testified. Seventeen-year-old John Brown had worked at the timber yard at the same time as Kirkpatrick and Lavelle. He told the inquest that Kirkpatrick had often tormented Lavelle, throwing chips at him and calling him an 'Irish pig.' After one particular bout of bullying at work, Lavelle told Brown that Kirkpatrick's time on earth would be short. 'I'll be hung for him if he doesn't leave me alone' he threatened.

The inquest returned a verdict of wilful murder against Michael Lavelle, who was committed for trial before Mr Justice Day at the forthcoming Liverpool Assizes, which opened on 15 February. There the case for the prosecution was outlined by Mr Shand, who described the events of 1 February that led up to Kirkpatrick's death.

Mr Justice Day (author's collection)

William Roberts described what had taken place in the timber yard and his recollections of witnessing the assault on Kirkpatrick. 'I did not mean to strike him, sir' interjected Lavelle.

Like the deceased and the accused, Roberts had formerly worked at Tickle's and he told the court that Kirkpatrick constantly bullied Lavelle. John Brown confirmed Roberts's testimony, recalling Kirkpatrick throwing chips at Lavelle's head and calling him an Irish pig and an Irish sow, telling the boy that his recently deceased mother was now in hell. Brown was followed by several other employees at Tickle's, who also deposed to the ill-treatment received by Lavelle at Kirkpatrick's hands. As well as constantly taunting him, Kirkpatrick had supposedly hit him, kicked him and choked him by pulling his muffler. Foreman Hugh Wilson described Lavelle as a quiet, inoffensive and very obliging young lad, adding that he appeared to be in a constant state of terror about Kirkpatrick. William Tickle himself stated that Lavelle was in his employ for two months and bore a good character. Tickle confirmed that there had been several complaints made to him about Kirkpatrick bullying the younger employees and it was also reported to him that Kirkpatrick had been ill-treating the defendant.

For the defence, Dr Commins M.P. referred to the case as a very miserable one from beginning to end. According to Commins, Kirkpatrick had been both a bully and a coward and, while Lavelle was no doubt exasperated by his ill-treatment, nobody could have imagined that a blow struck by such a slight, feeble boy could have proved fatal for a strong, powerful man. Aside from remarks made to John Brown in the heat of the moment there was nothing in the evidence that could lead the jury to believe that Lavelle had any murderous intent and he suggested that, at worst, Lavelle might be guilty of the lesser offence of manslaughter.

In summary, Mr Justice Day told the jury that he found it very painful to see a young lad who had hitherto borne an excellent character placed in the position he now occupied. However, it was Day's job to administer the law, regardless of how he felt. He had to assume that persons intended the natural consequences of their acts. If, under grave provocation, a person used a stick or a knife that he had in his hand at the time, the case would be one of manslaughter not murder. Yet while he recognised that there was a degree of provocation in this case, it was distant – at least two weeks had lapsed between the last incidence of bullying and the fatal assault on the bully. In this instance, the evidence of this provocation tended to indicate malice and a desire for revenge, which prohibited the reduction of the offence to manslaughter. In short, if the jury were of the opinion that the prisoner intended to inflict grievous bodily harm, he was guilty of wilful murder and it was their duty to bring in a verdict in accordance with the law, however painful that might be.

The jury retired for thirty minutes to consider their verdict, returning to pronounce Michael Lavelle guilty of murder, albeit with a strong recommendation to mercy. Lavelle, who had wept bitterly throughout the trial sobbed even louder. 'I did not intend to kill the man' he shouted.

Mr Justice Day placed the black cap on his head and commended the jury for doing their duty and returning an honest verdict. 'Do not be unduly buoyed up by the kind recommendation to mercy which the jury have made on your behalf and which I shall at once forward to the proper authorities, where I am sure it will receive the most earnest consideration' he warned Lavelle. 'Do not fail at once to prepare yourself, with the assistance that will be provided for you, for that great change to which it is now my duty to sentence you. The sentence is not my sentence but that which I am compelled by law to pass upon you' Day concluded, before sentencing Lavelle to death.

The sentence provoked a flood of outraged letters to the local newspapers, among them one from a member of the jury. They pointed out that, in front of witnesses, Kirkpatrick had done everything in his power to irritate and annoy Lavelle, particularly by trading on the youth's religious beliefs to outrage the memory of his dead mother. Being so much younger, smaller and frailer than the victim, Lavelle stood no chance of thrashing him in a fair fight. He therefore struck him a single, unlucky blow – one that, according to doctors, should have caused nothing more than a minor injury.

The only evidence of intent was the remark Lavelle made to John Brown: 'I'll be hung for him if he doesn't leave me alone.' Many people used similar expressions without thinking about what they really meant – if the lad had said 'I'll be damned…' instead of 'I'll be hung…' nobody would have thought to enter it as evidence of premeditation.

It came as no surprise when Lavelle's death sentence was commuted to one of life imprisonment. He was sent from Kirkdale Gaol in Liverpool to H.M.P. Gillingham and from there to Portland Prison in Dorset. On 15 August 1897, it was announced that the Secretary of State had agreed to Lavelle's release.

Yet within four months, Lavelle found himself at the Liverpool Assizes again, this time before Mr Justice Ridley. He was accused of causing grievous bodily harm to a man named Henry Sloane. After leaving prison, Lavelle found a job but was quickly fired and came to believe that Sloane was responsible for getting him dismissed. Although there was no foundation for this supposition, on 7 November, Lavelle sought out Sloane at his job as a night watchman and attacked him with a broom handle. Sloane was said to be 'a cripple' and was thus unable to defend himself against the unprovoked assault. Soon, Lavelle abandoned the broomstick and picked up a crowbar, with which he inflicted serious injuries, until eventually Sloane managed to pick up a metal bucket and put it over his head to deflect the rain of blows.

Arrested and charged with wounding, Lavelle told the police that he had only been released from Portland Prison four months ago and had been made 'daft' there. He now knew himself to be a lunatic. He claimed that Sloane had taunted him about being a prisoner and got him the sack but in spite of this he had never intended to hurt him and was very sorry for what he had done.

As twenty-eight-year-old Lavelle stood before the judge, his defence counsel Mr Segar informed the court that he believed that Lavelle was not in a fit state of mind, either to plead or to stand trial for the attack on Sloane. Nevertheless, bearing in mind his recent death sentence, his friends and relatives were anxious that he should be placed somewhere secure, where he could do no more harm. The judge took advice from Dr Price, the medical officer at Walton Prison, who conceded that Lavelle was of weak intellect and was subject to delusions. He was also subject to violent impulses without adequate cause but, in the doctor's opinion, Lavelle was well able to appreciate the difference between guilty and not guilty.

Having given details of the attack on Sloane, prosecuting Counsel Mr Mansfield told the jury that it would be up to them to determine whether they believed Lavelle capable of distinguishing right from wrong.

The defence called just one witness, Dr Price. The doctor agreed that Lavelle's delusions of persecution could be regarded as dangerous.

'Did he know that what he did was right or wrong? Did he know the difference? ' interjected the judge testily.

'I should think that he knew' replied Price.

Mr Justice Ridley (author's collection)

Mr Segar did not make a speech for the defence, leaving the judge to address the court. 'In this case, some persons seem to have got it into their heads that the prisoner is a lunatic' he began 'but the law is that he is responsible unless he was deficient in mind to such an extent so as not to know the quality and nature of the act he was committing. In 1886, the prisoner was convicted of murder at the Liverpool Assizes and sentenced to death. He wasn't spared because he was a lunatic but for some reason or other he was reprieved by the Home Secretary and the sentence was commuted to one of penal servitude for life. I do not see what evidence there is to find the prisoner insane' he stressed, before dismissing the jury to consider their verdict.

Broadmoor Criminal Lunatic Asylum, 1906 (author's collection)

When the jury found Lavelle guilty, the judge sentenced him to twelve months' hard labour, as well as the resumption of his previous life sentence. Lavelle was sent to Parkhurst Prison on the Isle of Wight but on 18 October 1898, he was certified insane and transferred to Broadmoor Criminal Lunatic Asylum. He is believed to have died there in 1913, aged forty-three.

'I did not think he had the heart to kill a mouse.'

Watford, Hertfordshire, 1889.

Joseph Taynton carried out his business as a shoe and bootmaker from his home at 1 South Terrace, Vicarage Road in Watford. On 8 April 1889, Taynton worked long into the evening, finally finishing at 8.40 p.m., at which time he had to go out on business. He stayed in town until around 9.30 p.m., after which he treated himself to a drink at the Liberal Club. When he arrived home at 10.50 a.m., he found his house full of police officers and his wife, Caroline, sitting in a chair, cradling the dead body of their ten-year-old daughter, Jessie Maria.

Joseph was unable to comprehend what was happening, having left a peaceful family home and returned to a scene of carnage. Two hours earlier, six-year-old Tommy was sleeping peacefully in his bed, while ten-year-old Jessie and fifteen-year-old Walter Joseph were sitting amicably together in the kitchen, she knitting, he reading.

When Joseph left home, Caroline was already out at a temperance meeting. When she left at 7.45 p.m., Joseph was working in the kitchen, Jessie was upstairs putting Tommy to bed and Walter was reading. Caroline came home at exactly 10.00 p.m. but found the door locked against her. She went round to the back of the house and knocked and called at the door but there was no response and, thinking that she could hear moaning coming from the kitchen, Caroline went to her next door neighbour for help. Alfred George Williams managed to gain entry to the house through the wash house window and unlocked the front door from the inside.

Caroline found Jessie lying on her back in the kitchen, surrounded by her father's tools, which were scattered all around her on the floor. The little girl's face was covered in blood and there was a large, spreading pool of blood by her head. Jessie was still clutching her knitting needles, on which the stocking she was knitting appeared undisturbed.

Jessie was alive and, although unconscious, she was groaning continuously. Caroline ran upstairs to find Walter, to ask him to go and find his father but he was not there. So, while Mr Williams went for a doctor, Caroline lifted her daughter onto her lap and tried to comfort her.

Surgeon Alfred Edward Cox arrived within minutes. Jessie was deathly pale and very cold, her hair full of blood and brain matter. As Cox examined her, she moved her lips just once before dying in her mother's arms. Cox noted three puncture wounds just above and in front of her right ear and a large depressed skull fracture measuring five by four inches and covering almost the whole of the right-hand side of her head. Near the middle of the room, a shoemaker's hammer lay on the floor, its head covered with blood and hair. Cox was certain that this hammer was the instrument responsible for Jessie's catastrophic head injuries. The wounds could not possibly have been self- inflicted, nor could they have been caused by an accidental fall onto the hammer. 'Fetch the police; this child has been murdered' he ordered Williams.

Superintendent Hummerstone duly arrived and, after consulting with Dr Cox, he went outside to look for Walter. He spotted the boy walking nonchalantly up Vicarage Road from the direction of the church and escorted him, into the house telling him that he intended to charge him with the wilful murder of his sister. The policeman noted that there were two wet patches at the bottom of Walter's waistcoat that looked as if they had been recently washed. Walter made no comment, appearing unmoved as he was taken to the police station, where a closer inspection revealed blood on his right shirt sleeve, thumb nail and on his jacket, near the shoulder.

Coroner Mr R.W. Brabant held an inquest on Jessie's death at the Watford Police Station on 9 April, at which the jury returned an open verdict, finding that Jessie died from her wounds but that there was insufficient evidence to show by whom those wounds were inflicted.

The next day, Caroline and Joseph Taynton went to see their son at the police station.

'How are you?' Caroline asked him awkwardly.

'Quite well'

'Are you sorry?'

'Yes' replied Walter

'Was it an accident?'

'No' he confirmed.

'Did you sleep well at the police station?' Once again, Walter's reply was a monosyllabic 'Yes'.

'I didn't sleep well' Caroline told him, but he didn't seem to register his mother's remark.

Joseph asked Walter to explain what had happened, saying that he was breaking his mother's heart.

'I shan't' he replied defiantly.

Mrs Taynton asked Walter if he would like to see his little sister and his only response was to nod his head in the affirmative. She handed her son two oranges she had bought for him and kissed him goodbye.

On 16 April, Walter appeared before magistrates at the Watford Police Court, charged with the wilful murder of his sister, showing no emotion whatsoever as he listened to the evidence against him. Only after he had been committed to appear at the Assizes did he show any sort of interest in his situation, asking PC Foster when his sister was due to be buried. When Foster told him that he believed that the funeral had been arranged for 20 April, Walter said conversationally 'She might have been alive now if she hadn't kept nagging me.' He then continued to tell Foster: 'I hit her with the hammer and she fell down. I do not know how many times I hit her when she was down. I lost my temper.'

Walter Taynton appeared before Lord Chief Justice Coleridge at the Hertfordshire Assizes, which opened on 1 August 1889. Mr Grubbe and Mr Wedderburn prosecuted and The Honourable Mr S. Holland acted in defence.

One of the first witnesses was Caroline Taynton, who described attending her temperance meeting and returning to find her daughter dying on the floor. She told the court that, before she left, Jessie and Walter seemed very friendly – more so than usual - although there was never really any ill-feeling between them, apart from normal childish squabbles.

Caroline told the court that Walter had always been a rather strange boy, who loved reading but had never passed a single year when he was at school. Describing her son as '…very dull and stupid', Caroline explained that he had a couple of fits as a toddler and now suffered from severe headaches, which would make him cry like a baby. According to Caroline, Walter had never mastered the art of dressing himself properly and even at fifteen years old, still had to be helped to put his braces on the right way. It was also very difficult to persuade him to wash. 'I never thought anything of this kind would happen' Caroline wept. 'I did not think he had the heart to kill a mouse.'

Walter was a solitary child, who shunned the company of other boys, preferring to read. (Shortly before killing his sister, he was engrossed in a book called '*Ceylon and its Dependencies*'). Often Walter would sit by the fire, his face contorting in involuntary grimaces and he would sometimes rub his hand on the sooty chimney and then deliberately blacken his face.

Although Joseph had tried to teach Walter the rudiments of the shoe making trade, he had failed dismally, as the boy couldn't grasp even the simplest of tasks. Yet Caroline confirmed that Walter loved playing with his father's tools and that she often had to stop him from using them at nights when Joseph finished work, for fear of disturbing the neighbours.

Joseph Taynton corroborated his wife's evidence, confirming for the jury that his own uncle died in a lunatic asylum and he also had an aunt who drowned herself.

The court then heard from Dr Cox, neighbour Mr Williams and police officers Hummerstone and Foster, who recorded Walter's confession. The next witness to be called was Thomas Gardiner, a headmaster for more than thirty years, who taught Walter during the six years he attended school. 'In the whole of that time, he never passed a single standard properly' testified Gardiner, describing Walter as the dullest boy in the school. Over the years, he had thousands of boys in his care yet had never met one who behaved in so strange a manner as Walter. He was frequently unable to comprehend what was said to him and would react to quite ordinary observations with a vacant stare.

Gardiner was convinced that Walter was insane, citing the boy's fondness for reading as being one of the signs. Dr Savage, a lecturer on mental diseases at Guy's Hospital told the court that he had asked Walter why he committed the deed and was told that it was because Jessie frequently teased him and, on the night of her death, had enraged him by calling him 'boss eye.' Savage believed that Walter was '…of low mental power'. Taking into consideration the distant but direct insanity in the family, the convulsions in infancy, the dullness at school, the solitariness and peculiarity of this boy, his unlovable disposition, his badly shaped head and the act itself, Savage was adamant that the boy was incapable of knowing right from wrong. To a lay mind, it appeared as though the fits at an early age would not have any ill effect on Walter but, in reality, they often hindered brain development.

The boy's odd conduct, the evidence of his mother about his strangeness and the assertions by his father that he was incapable of learning a trade, not to mention the evidence of the schoolmaster all served to confirm the correctness of this diagnosis, argued Savage. It was quite consistent with insanity that Walter should not remember what he had done. There was insanity without delusions and, while there was obviously a permanent weak-mindedness about Walter, there would probably be occasions when the insanity might either be more pronounced or might even decrease. As far as Walter's family history, insane tendencies often skipped a generation, so the want of development of Walter's brain was probably due to the insanity of his progenitors.

Another doctor, Dr Bates, had interviewed Walter twice and told the court that the boy had never shown any signs of insanity in his presence. He was quite able to differentiate between right and wrong and, although he was undoubtedly very quick tempered and prone to anger at the slightest provocation, the fact of a lad losing his temper was no indicator of insanity.

Mr Holland spoke for the defence, asking the jury to stifle their natural feelings of horror at this terrible case and resist the urge for revenge. The law was very clear, continued Holland. If anyone commits a crime at the time his brain was in such a diseased condition that he could not distinguish between right and wrong, the law stepped in and said he may be excused from punishment on the grounds of insanity.

As for motive, there simply did not seem to be a satisfactory one in this case. The children were living together in a happy home, with loving parents and surroundings of an eminently happy character. Both the prisoner and his sister were of good character and on this particular evening, they seemed loving but then he suddenly killed her. He did not then do what a lad would normally do on realising the awful crime he has committed but simply went out and returned an hour later, seemingly oblivious to what had taken place.

It seemed to Holland that there were numerous indicators of insanity in this boy, not to mention in his ancestors. If the jury could not accept the theory of insanity, he asked them seriously if they could really believe that there was a boy on God's earth so horribly cruel, so utterly bad, such a devil, as to kill his little sister, whom he loved, in cold blood. This horrible crime was done on the spur of the moment and was evidently not premeditated, for if it had been, would not the deed have been committed at the earliest opportunity and in a place where there would be a greater probability of mysterious surroundings to baffle inquiry into the case than in his own home, where he must have known he would be speedily discovered?

It was left to the judge to sum up the case and his first point was that there was the clearest possible proof that Jessie Taynton was murdered by her brother. There were therefore only three questions for the jury to consider: did the prisoner commit the act with the full intention of committing it as an ordinary, reasonable being and was he therefore guilty of wilful murder? Did he commit the act under circumstances that might warrant the jury finding him guilty of manslaughter? Or did he commit the act in such circumstances that would enable them to find that he was in such a state of mind at the time through insanity that he was not responsible for his actions?

The law presumed that if one man took away another's life intentionally, then he was guilty of murder, continued Coleridge. Provocation by words did not reduce this to manslaughter, the law holding that a blow must first be struck before the jury might consider a verdict of manslaughter. If the jury thought that the evidence showed this little girl guilty of such provocation, they could return a verdict of manslaughter or alternatively, if they believed that the prisoner was unable at the time to distinguish between right and wrong, they could return a verdict to that effect. However, he must caution them that a verdict of not guilty on the grounds of insanity may result in the prisoner being shut up for life.

It took the jury just fifteen minutes to return a verdict that Walter Joseph Taynton was guilty of manslaughter and, after due consideration, the judge awarded a sentence of ten years' penal servitude. Having taken no apparent interest in the case throughout, Taynton showed no reaction whatsoever to the sentence.

Official records show that in 1891, Walter was an inmate at H.M. Convict Prison, Guston, in Kent, which closed in 1895. It has proved difficult to trace his whereabouts after this, although a man named 'Walt Taynton', who was born in 1874, apparently immigrated to Canada on 18 March 1897.

'We did it for to steal his clothes'.

Liverpool, 1891.

The Junior Reform Club had commissioned new premises on the corner of Stanley Street and Victoria Street in Liverpool. However, shortly after construction began, the Junior Conservative Club went into liquidation and so the Reformers took over their premises and simply abandoned their proposed new building. By 1891, seven years later, the site was little more than waste land and although it was surrounded by hoardings, it proved a magnet to the local children, who simply scrambled over or through the barriers to play football and generally mess about. There were several large shallow pools of water on the site and the children often paddled, bathed or sailed makeshift rafts there.

On 8 September 1891, sixteen-year-old Robert McGibbon was walking down Stanley Street. Several boys were playing football on the building site but as McGibbon walked past a gap in the fencing he thought he saw a child lying face down in one of the pools. McGibbon paused for a closer look then ran for a policeman.

PC Horrocks hurried to the scene and pulled the body of a young boy from the water. Awaiting the arrival of medical assistance, Horrocks attempted artificial respiration but when Dr Williams from the Northern Hospital arrived, he told the policeman that the boy had been dead for some time. All efforts to resuscitate the child were abandoned and the body was taken to the Prince's Lock mortuary.

As soon as the news of the child's death was made public, a steady stream of parents visited the mortuary in search of missing boys. One, Mrs Elizabeth Dawson Eccles, identified the dead child as her son, David. She told the police that David was eight-and-a-half years old and had been '... a bit unmanageable of late', occasionally playing truant and sleeping rough rather than returning to his home in Richmond Row. Mrs Eccles told the police that she last saw her son on 7 September, when he left home after eating his lunch to walk back to Bevington Bush School. At the time, he was wearing a corduroy suit with a cap, a scarf, a shirt and laced boots but when pulled from the water he was completely naked and there was no sign of his clothes

It was initially assumed that David had drowned while bathing and that he had probably removed his clothes before entering the water. However, once details of David's tragic death were published in the local evening newspaper, a woman named Mary Shearan went to the police station.

Mary's real name was Mary O'Brien but she and her illegitimate son Robert went by the name of the man she cohabited with in Baptist Street. Like David Dawson Eccles, eight-year-old Robert had recently been somewhat unmanageable and on 7 September, he arrived home at 10.30 a.m. having not been home for the previous two days and nights. Mary gave her son breakfast and sent him to bed, taking away all of his clothes, which were in need of washing. She then left the house for twenty minutes and, when she returned, Robert had gone wearing nothing more than a piece of old sacking and a child's ragged dress. When he finally arrived home again at 11.00 p.m., Robert was wearing a corduroy suit, identical in description to that reported to have been worn by the deceased child. As Mary undressed her son to put him to bed, she asked him where he got the clothes from and he told her that he had found them at the 'rafts' in Victoria Street.

When Mary read about David's clothes, she asked her son again where he had got the corduroy suit. Although Robert stuck to his story, his mother didn't believe him and threatened him with a thrashing if he didn't tell the truth. When Robert eventually told her 'Me and Sammy Crawford threw the boy in the rafts' she went to the police.

Detective James Spence went to Baptist Road to speak to Robert and asked him about the clothes that Mary took to the detective's office. 'Crawford gave him a push as well as me' protested Robert.

'Gave who a push?' asked Spence.

'The boy in the pit' answered Robert.

When Spence went to interview nine-year-old Samuel Crawford, he claimed that his friend Robert had pushed the boy into the water. Spence took Samuel to the police station, where, having been officially cautioned, the child made a statement: 'I am nine years of age and live at 1 house, 2 Court, Baptist Street. About seven o'clock on Monday night the 7th Shearan came to me at St George's Hall with the boy. We asked him to go to the rafts. He said "Where is it?" We told him in Victoria Street. It was just seven o'clock when we got there. We got over the hoarding in Cumberland Street. There were three or four office boys there. We waited until they went away. We asked him to go on a plank and he would not because he was afraid. We then pushed him in. We dragged him out, dragged his clothes off and pushed him in again. He fell on his right side, face downwards. We then took his clothes and went away. Shearan got his shirt and trousers and coat and gave me his vest. We put his socks into his boots and threw them in the pit. His cap and tie we threw into the pit. We did it for to steal his clothes. We then went away.'

Spence escorted Samuel to Victoria Street and he pointed out where he and Robert had disposed of the boots, cap and tie. The boots were found exactly where Samuel indicated but the cap and tie were never found. Robert Shearan was then cautioned and he too made a remarkably similar statement: 'I am eight years of age and live at 25 Baptist Street. I met the boy about two o'clock on Monday the 7th in Great Charlotte Street. I took him to St George's Hall, where I met Crawford. We then went to the rafts in Victoria Street. I got over the hoarding first. Then Crawford lifted the boy over the hoarding. There were some office boys in the pit. We waited till they had gone. We asked him to go on a plank but he would not. We then pushed him in and dragged him out again and dragged off his clothes and pushed him in again. He was scrambling out and we pulled him out of the water and pushed him in again. He fell on his right side, face downwards. Crawford then got onto his head with his knees and kept him under water for about five minutes. We waited till nine o'clock to see if he stirred. He never stirred. We then took his clothes. I took his coat, shirt and trousers and gave Crawford his vest. His boots, socks, tie and cap we threw into the pit. We wanted to steal his clothes.'

An inquest was opened and adjourned by coroner Mr Clarke Aspinall. When it finally concluded on 23 September, the jury had heard that Robert and Samuel had confessed to killing David Dawson Eccles and that both boys had returned home on the night of 7 September wearing articles of the dead boy's clothing. Several witnesses had seen Eccles with Robert Shearan during that afternoon and evening and told the inquest that the sighting of the two boys was particularly memorable since Robert was wearing only a piece of sacking. One witness, apprentice printer Walter Parkhouse had actually spoken to Robert and David and recalled Robert telling him that he lived in Baptist Street and that his trousers had been stolen from him. Parkhouse advised him to go to the Children's Shelter.

After hearing from Dr E. J. Foulston, who confirmed that David's death was caused by drowning, the inquest jury needed only a few minutes' deliberation to return a verdict of wilful murder against Robert Shearan and Samuel Crawford, who were committed to take their trial on the coroner's warrant and removed to the workhouse to await the start of the proceedings against them.

The trial opened before Mr Justice Lawrance at Liverpool Assizes on Wednesday 9 December 1891. The case was prosecuted by Mr

Hopwood QC and Mr Squarey and, at the request of the judge Mr Compton-Smith defended both boys.

SHEARON.   CRAWFORD.

Hopwood began by informing the jury that it would be their job to decide whether the two children in the dock had committed the murder with which they were charged and, if so, were they of sufficient capacity of mind to understand the nature of the act that they had committed. He then described the location of the tragedy, revealing that David had drowned in a pool of water less than 8½ inches deep that had gathered in a corner of what would have been the basement of the new building.

Robert McGibbon then spoke about spotting the body and fetching a policeman. He was followed into the witness box by Elizabeth Dawson Eccles, who recalled the last time she had seen her son alive and the clothes he was then wearing.

The policemen who had removed the body from the water and escorted it to the mortuary were next to testify, followed by witnesses who had seen David with the two defendants at the Victoria Street site.

Mary O'Brien then recounted taking her sons clothes for washing, only for him to escape from the house wrapped in a piece of old sacking. She told the court that after reading about David's death in the newspaper, she had taken the clothes her son had 'found' to the detective's office. There was some argument from the defence counsel about the timing of Robert's statement to the police, since his mother had threatened to thrash him if he didn't tell her the truth about where the clothes came from. However, Mary O'Brien swore that she had not threatened a thrashing until after Robert had told her that he and Samuel had pushed a boy into the water.

Caroline Crawford was also called to testify about her son's clothing. According to her evidence, on the day of the drowning, Samuel went out in his shirt sleeves and returned wearing an old jacket with no sleeves. When she questioned her son about the garment, he told her that a ragman had given it to him.

Detective James Spence gave evidence about interviewing both boys, adding that he had personally taken Crawford back to Victoria Street, where the boy revealed the exact location of David's missing boots. Mr Compton Smith cross-examined Spence on his recall of precisely what was said by the two boys. The detective denied having heard the boys say that David had slipped while running round the wall above the pit and also insisted that he had not heard the boys say that they had warmed themselves and dried the wet clothes at a street brazier behind the Bon Marché store or that they had been given a penny by a gentleman, which they used to buy chips. Spence insisted that he had not questioned the boys at all but merely taken down their statements. Compton Smith immediately asked him about Samuel's assertion that it was seven o'clock when the boys reached Victoria Street. 'I asked him how he knew the hour and he replied "Because the big clock was striking"' replied Spence.

'I thought you said you did not ask any questions.' Compton Smith remarked pointedly.

Chief Detective Inspector Irvine then stated that he had cautioned the two boys and was in attendance when they made their statements. He divulged that the statements were not written down at the time and that he was not present when the boys' words were transcribed.

The next witness was surgeon Edward James Postance, who had made a post-mortem examination of David Dawson Eccles that confirmed that the cause of his death was drowning. Describing David as a 'strong, healthy boy', Postance revealed that he had found abrasions on the body, which might have been inflicted before death. There were cuts on David's nose and a little blood on his brain, while his heart was strongly contracted, which Postance believed was consistent with David having received a shock from a fall. Postance then revised the cause of death to a combination of shock and drowning, which could conceivably be consistent with a fall from a wall into water.

After hearing from Postance, the prosecution rested, leaving the floor clear for defence counsel Mr Compton Smith. Telling the jury that he had actually visited the site where the drowning took place and spoken at length to both boys, Compton Smith said that his defence would be two-fold. In the first instance, he was of the opinion that the prosecution had not successfully proved that the boys committed the crime. However, even if the jury came to the conclusion that the charge had been substantially proved, each of the boys was under fourteen years of age and he therefore argued that, at the time, they were not conscious of the gravity of the act that they were perpetrating.

The first question to answer was had a murder been committed? Compton Smith asked the jury to consider the facts of the matter with the statements that it was alleged the boys had made. It would be impossible to convict a grown man on the evidence that the counsel for the prosecution had submitted to the court, contended Compton Smith. Recalling the medical evidence, he reminded the jury that the post-mortem examination had supported the theory that David Dawson Eccles had fallen from the wall into the water.

Compton Smith reminded the jury that none of the witnesses had seen the victim and the defendants together actually inside the hoardings at Victoria Street. Addressing Detective Spence's testimony, Compton Smith claimed that there were at least four falsehoods. Spence stated under oath that the statements were written down directly from the mouths of the prisoners but his superior gave lie to that statement, testifying that this was not true.

When asked by magistrates what they had to say about the charge against them, both boys had replied 'Nothing.' Compton Smith suggested that this is precisely what they would have said in answer to the Detective Spence.

There were words in the statements that two young boys simply would not have used, maintained Compton Smith, who also pointed out the remarkable similarity between the two statements, giving as an example the inclusion of the same phrase' He fell on his right side, face downwards' in both. However, according to the evidence given by Detectives Spence and Irvine, the boys had been together while making their statements, so a certain amount of similarity was to be expected.

Furthermore, Compton Smith insisted that a 'guilty mind' had not been proven and he submitted that it was incumbent on the prosecution to prove that the boys had a guilty knowledge of the likely results of their actions. He suggested that the boys had no idea that their deeds could cause death – he did not imagine that they had ever seen a dead man or that they even knew what death was. Both boys had been brought up in the lowest area of the city, living in houses 'infested' with prostitutes and thieves. They had been given no instruction on moral or religious life and had been brought up in misery and want.

Mr Justice Lawrance (author's collection)

Mr Justice Lawrance then summed up the case for the jury. He instructed them that the law presumed that a person under the age of seven could not be guilty of the crime of murder and that between the ages of seven and fourteen, a person could be guilty of murder only if the prosecution could satisfactorily prove that he or she was aware of the nature and quality of the act committed.

Until statements were made by the two boys, in spite of the fact that he was in possession of an item of David's clothing, there was nothing to incriminate Samuel Crawford in the murder, whereas Shearan had at least been seen in the company of the victim. Referring to the evidence given by Detective Spence, Lawrance described the testimony about the boys' statements as 'misleading'. Spence's testimony led the court to believe that Crawford's statements were all made on one day and that Spence took down those statements in the presence of Detective Irvine. Yet Irvine stated that he had not seen the statements written down, which now threw doubt upon Spence's assertion that the boys were together when they made their statements.

The judge mused that the evidence against Shearan was far stronger than that against Crawford – in fact he believed it so strong that, were the defendant an adult, there could only really be one verdict. However, the judge wondered aloud if the evidence against Crawford was quite as conclusive? However, if the jury believed that both boys had a hand in the death of David Dawson Eccles, they must consider whether the defendants understood the terrible seriousness of their crimes.

The jury retired for ninety minutes, returning to pronounce both defendants guilty of the act but not responsible, owing to their tender age. This amounts to a verdict of 'not guilty' ruled the judge, although he ordered that the boys should not be liberated immediately, announcing his intention to try and get them into an institution, where they would be cared for.

The jury's decision did not sit well with many of the contemporary newspapers, some of which had already billed the case 'the ghastliest murder on record', on the grounds that 'murdered and murderers, all three were infants.' *The Pall Mall Gazette* asked 'What is it in the dreary annals of murder that makes one crime stand out among its fellows? Is it inadequacy of motive? Pitiful inadequacy of motive is here. Cold, savage deliberation in committing the crime? Horror and cruelty in the circumstances of its accomplishment? Such deliberation, such cruelty, was never more revoltingly displayed than here.' Describing Shearan and Crawford as 'ruffians', 'fiends' and 'wretched butchers', the newspapers seemed most affronted by the calm, calculating way in which David Dawson Eccles was tormented by being dragged out of the water and having his clothes removed, before being cast back into the water naked and deliberately drowned. That his supposed killers then sat watching to make absolutely sure that they had '…stamped out the last spark of life' only added to '…the pity and terror of it.'

Note: There are several variations in names in the contemporary newspapers. The youth who first spotted David's body is named as Robert McGibbon and Robert McGiveron. Robert Shearon is also named Sheeran, Shearan, Sheernan and O'Brien.

'Now I shall be hung.'

Portland, Dorset, 1891.

The naval training ship *H.M.S. Boscawen* first arrived in Portland in 1862, replacing *H.M.S. Britannia*, which then moved from Portland to Dartmouth in Devon to become the forerunner of the Royal Naval College. The original *Boscawen* was replaced in 1873 by *H.M.S. Trafalgar,* which subsequently adopted the name *Boscawen* and remained in Portland until 1906, when she was sold.

H.M.S. Boscawen (author's collection)

Life on a naval training ship in the nineteenth century was not easy for the boys on board, being taught the many and varied tasks they would have to tackle as men at sea. They learned the rudiments of reading and writing, along with how to set rigging, use rifles, clean and maintain the ship, scrub and wash hammocks and make and mend clothes. They also took part in a punishing schedule of physical exercises and gymnastics. Fire being a great danger in a wooden ship at sea, the boys formed a fire brigade, which, in emergencies, could be called on to assist with fires on land. On Sundays, every boy was expected to attend divine service. Discipline on the ship was harsh and, in 1866, it is recorded that two boys each received 24 lashes from the birch.

By 1891, there were 549 boys on board the *Boscawen*, most aged between twelve and seventeen years old, with each boy receiving weekly pocket money of around 3d. As the boys were often prevented from leaving the ship for long periods, due to bad weather or an infectious illness, for which the entire ship was quarantined, life on board could be confining and claustrophobic.

On Sunday 15 November 1891, after attending the religious services, three of the *Boscawen* boys obtained permission to go ashore. Together they walked along the top of the cliffs at Portland towards Bow and Arrow Castle, enjoying a rare chance to stretch their legs, chatting and picking blackberries as they went.

One boy, William Groom, was about thirty yards ahead of the other two, half listening to their conversation about the Shambles lightship, a vessel that warned other ships about the treacherous Shambles sandbar between Weymouth and Portland. Suddenly, what Groom later described as a 'groan' interrupted the talking, and then the conversation behind him abruptly ceased. Turning round to see what had happened, Groom saw sailor John George Wise perched precariously on the edge of the one hundred foot high cliffs on his hands and knees, peering over the top and laughing loudly. Groom rushed to see what was going on and, as he looked over the cliff, he spotted 'a bundle of blue' at the bottom and realised that it was the third boy, Lawrence Salter.

Children playing in the gardens of the nearby prison cottages had seen Salter fall and raised the alarm. A party of rescuers descended the cliffs, finding Salter still alive but terribly injured. He was brought carefully to the top and taken to the prison infirmary, where he died half an hour later.

Groom asked Wise if he had pushed Salter, but Wise made no reply, just continued to laugh maniacally, so much so that his legs would no longer support him and he fell to the ground. By now, all the frightened Groom could think was to get Wise back to the Boscawen. He seized Wise's hands, pulled him upright and began to walk him towards the ship. However, on their way back, they met one of the ship's officers, petty officer first-class Benjamin Stuckey, and, to his relief, Groom was able to hand Wise over into his charge after telling the officer that he wished to report Wise because he believed that he had pushed Salter over the cliff. Wise immediately confessed to Stuckey that he had indeed done exactly that - he had deliberately pushed Salter over the cliff in order to get hanged.

Doubting that Wise could be in his right mind, Stuckey asked the boy if there was anything the matter with him, to which Wise replied that he was subject to 'fits of frenzy' and that he must have killed Salter in one of those fits.

Back on board the *Boscawen*, Wise repeated this statement to Lieutenant Andrew Stafford Mills, saying that he had gone ashore with the sole intention of killing somebody. 'I tried to settle one last leave and I have succeeded this time', he cheerfully told Mills, continuing to smile or laugh all the while he was being questioned and apparently taking great delight in repeatedly proclaiming 'Now I shall be hung.'

An inquest was opened on the death of Lawrence Salter on 17 November, at The Grove Inn, Portland, before Coroner Sir Richard Howard. William Eliot Stone told the inquest that he had been walking on the cliffs with his seven-year-old daughter Mabel when Salter fell. The three *Boscawen* boys passed them, asking Stone what the time was, then minutes later Salter fell over the cliff.

Stone rushed to assist him, finding the boy lying at the cliff bottom, groaning and complaining of pain in his arm and back. 'Oh, help me, help me' he begged Stone. Realising that one of the boy's arms was badly broken, Stone bound it up, before fetching some water and carefully washing the blood from the boy's face, comforting him until the stretcher party arrived. Salter was conveyed to the infirmary at Portland Prison, where he died from serious brain injuries, resulting from a fracture at the base of his skull.

Wise smiled throughout, even as the coroner's jury recorded a verdict of wilful murder against him. At this, he was arrested and remanded in Dorchester prison. The very next day, he was brought before Mr Justice Cave at the Dorset Assizes but the judge was not prepared to hear the case, since the alleged murder had happened less than a week before and Wise had not yet been before magistrates. Describing Wise as a poor, friendless boy, Cave warned against pressing on with the case too hastily. In fairness, he said, Wise should be permitted to have witnesses for his defence and, since there were questions about his sanity, he also deserved the benefit of medical opinion.

John Wise duly appeared before magistrates at Dorchester on 11 December 1891. Mr Howard Bowen prosecuted the case and Wise was not defended, although it was noted that he was in the hands of a medical expert who would give evidence at 'the proper time'. During his confinement, Wise had voluntarily made a written statement, which was read aloud by the Magistrates' Clerk. 'On Sunday 15th November, I, John Wise, Lawrence Salter and William Groom were walking along the cliffs. Salter asked me to show him The Shambles lighthouse. I showed it to him with the words 'Do you see that point?' He said 'Do you feel that point?' and, at the same time, stuck a pin in my leg. I shoved him away from me and he slipped and fell headlong over the cliff. I turned round to see where he was. He was just going over. I tried to grasp him but it was too late. I was then seized with a fit of laughter, like an imbecile. Groom came up and said 'Where is Salter? What have you done with him?' A mad feeling then came over me and when I tried to speak to Groom fire danced before my eyes and I fell down. Groom took me by the wrist and led me away. We went towards the ship but did not meet anyone till we got near the pier. We then met a coxswain, whom Groom told about the matter. He asked me whether it was true that I had pushed Salter over the cliff. I said yes and that I had done it in order to get hanged. He then gave me in charge of an instructor, who brought me on board. At the inquest I was quite calm. When it was all over, Lieutenant Mills then asked me about it and I told him the truth; that I never intended to throw Salter over the cliff. I make this statement, which I declare to be the whole truth JOHN GEORGE WISE.'

Wise was committed for trial at the next assizes and, by the time the trial opened before Mr Justice Wills at Dorchester on 7 March 1892, extensive investigations had been made into both his medical history and his current state of mind. Mr M.W. McKellar and Mr Evelyn Cecil prosecuted the case and, by now, Mr A Cardew had been appointed as defence counsel.

The court heard accounts of the events of the day of the murder, followed by evidence from the master-at-arms of the *Boscawen*. Robert Franklin told the court that Salter, a native of West Ealing, London, had celebrated his sixteenth birthday on the day before his death. He had joined the *Boscawen* on 16 September 1891 and was 'well conducted', as indeed was Wise.

Wise was sixteen and a half years old at the time of Salter's death and had seven months service. During that time he had tried to commit suicide by swallowing oxalic acid. On 23 July 1891, he had boasted to his crewmates that, before joining the ship, he had strangled a young boy at Croydon and buried him behind the Roman Catholic school. When it was suggested that he was delusional, he had assured people that he wished he could think so, but sadly he knew it to be true. He was so convinced that he was a killer that, while on shore at Portland, he once handed himself in to the local police, making a statement that gave extensive details about the name of the victim, the location of the murder and the site where the body was buried. After investigating Wise's claims, Croydon police telegraphed their Dorset colleagues to inform them that the murder was merely a figment of his fevered imagination. He was taken before magistrates and given a severe telling off but continued to insist that he was a murderer.

Mentally, Wise was a very troubled young man. Witnesses described him as having been 'eccentric' ever since he was a child of eight years old and his father and several other relatives had died in lunatic asylums. Although he had now changed his account of the events surrounding the death of Salter to say that the young sailor's death had been an accident, Wise had assured everyone prior to his trial that he had no personal grudge against his victim but had just seized the opportunity to kill him. There had been no scuffling or fighting, just one swift push. Wise had also said that he did not dislike being in the navy but that he would just as soon be out of this world than in it.

Mr Justice Wills (author's collection)

The jury retired only briefly before returning with their verdict, finding John Wise guilty of the wilful murder of Lawrence Salter but stating that he was insane at the time of the killing. Ironically for a boy who, by his own account, had committed murder specifically so that he might be hanged, Mr Justice Wills directed that Wise should be detained as a criminal lunatic in Dorchester Prison until her Majesty's pleasure should be known. Wise was sent to Broadmoor Criminal Lunatic Asylum, where he died from bronchitis in March 1903.

'I never, I never, I never, done such a thing.'

Hackney, London, 1893.

Solicitor Solomon Myers lived on Amhurst Road, Dalston, Hackney, with his wife, Rosa, and their five children, Harry (8), Jonas (6), Esther (4½), Solomon junior (22 months) and a nine-month-old baby girl named Ray Maud. The Myers family employed three servants – a general servant, Beatrice Clark, nursery governess Lottie Bethell (or Bethel) and Emily Newber (or Neuber), who was employed as a nursery nurse to the three youngest children.

Fifteen-year-old Emily entered the household on Saturday 2 December 1893, after being interviewed by Rosa Myers for the vacant position of nursemaid, which was previously held by Beatrice Clark. Emily brought her mother with her to the interview and, when Mrs Myers expressed concern that the girl had no references from her previous employer, mother and daughter both assured her that this was because the woman had gone out of her mind. Mrs Myers believed them and Emily was given a week's trial.

On the evening of 8 December, Lottie Bethell brought the baby downstairs and Mrs Myers noticed that Ray's face was scratched and that her lips and eyes appeared swollen. Mrs Myers immediately went upstairs and questioned the three servants, all of whom denied knowing what was wrong with Ray. Since the infant was supposed to be in Emily's charge, Mrs Myers questioned her particularly stringently, asking if the baby had fallen or knocked herself but Emily insisted that she could offer no explanation for the marks on the baby's face.

The following morning marked the end of Emily's trial period and Mrs Myers decided to terminate her employment, on the grounds that she wasn't looking after the children carefully enough. On hearing that she was to be dismissed, Emily was distraught, sobbing loudly and begging to be allowed to stay, saying that she was afraid to go home and would be out on the streets if she was fired. Mrs Myers kindly offered to keep Emily on for another week, to give her a chance to find alternative employment, but she stressed to the girl that she could only stay for one more week, absolutely no longer.

On Sunday 10 December, Lottie Bethell went out, leaving Emily in sole charge of the children. At around 7.00 p.m., Mrs Myers checked to see that she was coping, finding Solomon and Ray asleep in their cots, in the room that they and Esther shared with Emily. Mrs Myers asked Emily to pop out for some bread and played with Esther downstairs while the nursemaid ran her errand, which took around five or six minutes. When Emily returned, she picked Esther up and carried her upstairs in her arms, while, having finished serving dinner, Beatrice Clark came to help put the two older boys to bed.

Within minutes, Mrs Myers became aware of baby Ray crying upstairs. She called out to ask Emily if she was there and, when Emily answered in the affirmative, she asked her to try and keep the baby quiet, suggesting that she stayed in the bedroom with her. Roughly twenty minutes later, Harry called out urgently 'Mamma, Mamma. Baby…'

Mrs Myers immediately shouted upstairs, asking Emily what was the matter with the baby and the nursemaid replied that the infant was choking and that there was white froth on its pillow. 'Bring her down quickly' Mrs Myers instructed and when Emily complied, Ray was foaming at the mouth and struggling to breathe, her lips swollen and her face purple. Mrs Myers told Beatrice Clark to run for the doctor, which she did. Meanwhile, Solomon Myers snatched the baby from his wife's arms. 'What have you been doing to this baby again?' he asked Emily, who replied 'Nothing, sir.'

'Go and get me the feeding bottle or any other bottles that you have in that room' Myers ordered and Emily raced upstairs and returned with a feeding bottle and a medicine bottle marked 'Spasmodic Mixture', which Myers put into his pocket, before hurrying to the doctor's with his daughter in his arms.

Beatrice and Mr and Mrs Myers arrived on the doctor's doorstep almost simultaneously. Surgeon William Henry Gimlet examined the baby, whose nightclothes smelled strongly of acetic acid and concluded that she had ingested corrosive poison and possibly also morphia. He administered something to neutralise the effects of the acid and also an emetic, which caused the baby to vomit. Gimlet told Mr and Mrs Myers to take the baby home and bathe it. Later that night, he called at their house to check on the child's condition, finding clear evidence of corrosive burns on the infant's lips and tongue. He advised Mr and Mrs Myers to take their daughter to the nearby German Hospital so that a tracheotomy could be performed.

Gimlet accompanied the family to the hospital and, once there, he drew the attention of house surgeon Joseph J. Bush to the child's contracted pupils and the strong smell of acetic acid on her breath. A tracheotomy was duly performed by Dr Josef Zambusch at around 3.00 a.m. on 11 December, but Ray died the following day. A post mortem examination showed that her tongue, palate, tonsils, gullet and stomach were all badly inflamed and corroded, the cause of her death being bronchial pneumonia. The house surgeon and Gimlet were of the opinion that baby Ray had ingested about a teaspoonful of glacial acetic acid, probably no more than half an hour before she was first seen at the doctor's surgery.

On their return from the hospital, Rosa Myers asked Emily for the baby's pillow, but Emily claimed that she couldn't find it. Mrs Myers went upstairs to look for it herself and found a small bottle in the room that Emily shared with the three youngest children. The bottle was clearly labelled 'Poison' and contained just a few drops of liquid. On seeing the bottle, Solomon Myers sent for the police and Sergeant George Childs arrived at the house at around 1.00 a.m. on 11 December. Childs interviewed Emily, who claimed to have been putting the other children to bed when she saw Beatrice Clark coming downstairs. When she heard the baby cry, Emily said that she had picked her up and rushed downstairs, saying 'Mistress, there is something the matter with the baby.'

Once Childs had left, Solomon Myers went to talk to Emily, who now swore that shortly before the baby began choking, she had seen Lottie crying in the nursery. Having been with the family for around six years, Lottie was considered 'a superior type of servant' and was therefore above suspicion, besides which Myers was positive that she was not in the house at the time of the incident, since he himself had let her back in at around 10.00 p.m. Later Emily told Beatrice Clark that she had seen Solomon junior in the nursery with a poison bottle in his hand.

Eventually, Emily approached Solomon Myers and confessed 'I want to tell you something. I did punch the baby about on the night of the 8th; I did punch it in the face and eyes, but I am sure I did not give it the poison.' Determined to get to the bottom of the matter, Mr Myers handed Emily and Beatrice each a piece of paper, telling them. 'There have been so many lies told yesterday; here are two pieces of paper; if you want to say anything further about the case you can write it down, and, you quite understand, after you have done so I shall hand them over to the police. Please yourselves whether you will do so or not. '

Emily continued to give differing accounts of what happened to the baby. She admitted that her statement that she had seen Solomon junior with the poison bottle was a lie but then claimed to have seen Beatrice feeding Ray something from a cup. When Mr Myers read her statement, he found that she had written: 'Baby was so cross that I slapped it on the face, but I can't say how the scratches came on her face. I got her to sleep, and came downstairs, and stayed in the kitchen till it was time to go to bed; and then, when Lottie saw the baby's face, she brought her downstairs to you. I had been playing in the front room with the children until mistress came up and looked at them, and then told me to get the water and wash them. I did so; I had washed Esther and started on Harry when mistress called me, and told me she wanted me to go on an errand, and I left the children and came downstairs. I went on the errand, and before I went up again nurse [Beatrice Clark] came down and went into the baby's room. I went up, and had hardly been upstairs three or four minutes when baby cried as usual, and then I heard mistress call me, and I went to the top of the staircase, and mistress asked me if I was up there, and I answered yes, and ran back to the baby, and found her as if she could not get her breath, and from her mouth came white stuff. I picked her up, and went to the top of the stairs and called mistress twice, and then Harry called, and then mistress called up to me, "Bring her down" and I done so; but as to anything else, I know nothing. That is all the truth.'

As he had promised, Mr Myers called the police again and when they arrived, Emily declared that she had forgotten to include something in her statement. She took back the piece of paper and added 'I went into the bedroom to get Esther the chamber, and I saw nurse [Beatrice Clark] giving the baby something out of a cup. I asked nurse what it was, and she said "milk"'.

Having now given five or six conflicting statements, Emily was arrested and charged with assault and also with administering poison with intent to do grievous bodily harm. After baby Ray's death, the charge of wilful murder was added to the list.

Deputy Coroner Alfred Hodgkinson held an inquest on the death of baby Ray and, having heard all of the evidence, the jury returned an open verdict, ruling that death was due to bronchial pneumonia, caused by the administration of a corrosive poison, adding that, in their opinion, there was nothing to show by whom it was administered.

In spite of the obvious doubts of the inquest jury, after several appearances at North London Police Court, Emily Newber was committed for trial on a charge of wilful murder. She appeared before Mr Justice Grantham at the Central Criminal Court on 5 February 1894.

Mr Justice Grantham (author's collection)

The first witness was Mr Myers, who gave details of the members of his household and where each person slept. He then went on to describe the mysterious injuries to his baby daughter's face, shortly followed by the child's poisoning, apparently by one of the family's servants. Myers recounted the various different statements made by Emily Newber and agreed that while he, his wife and Beatrice Clarke were at the doctor's surgery with the baby, Emily was alone in the house with the other four children and would have had ample opportunity to dispose of the incriminating poison bottle, if she wanted to do so.

It was established that the acetic acid had been purchased by Beatrice Clark many months earlier. Clark had used about half the acid to treat a wart on her face, before placing the bottle containing the remainder in a work basket, in her trunk.

On 8 December, Emily asked Beatrice to lend her an apron and Beatrice sent her to her bedroom on the top floor, telling her that she would find one in her trunk. At around the same time, Emily also asked Beatrice for some cotton and was again directed to help herself from Beatrice's trunk. On the day of the baby's poisoning, Beatrice asked Lottie to post a letter for her when she went out. Believing that she had a stamp in her trunk, Beatrice turned the contents out onto the floor but was unable to find one. The contents of the trunk were left scattered on the floor for the rest of the day and, as far as Beatrice was aware, remained undisturbed.

Beatrice told the court that there was some phosphorous paste in the house that was used to kill rats. When she and Emily were cleaning a shelf, Emily picked up the paste and asked Beatrice what it was for. When Beatrice explained, what it was, Emily was interested to find out whether or not it would poison anybody and Beatrice told her that it probably would.

Faced with Emily's assertion that she had given the baby something to drink out of a cup, Beatrice told the court that this was an absolute lie, as did Lottie Bethell, who was called to address Emily's story that she had been crying in the day nursery shortly before the baby was poisoned.

The court then heard medical evidence from William Gimlet, who was followed into the witness box by police sergeants George Childs and Richard Nursey. Childs spoke about taking Emily's initial statement and recalled collecting a bottle marked 'Poison' from Mrs Myers, which he later handed to Nursey, along with the baby's feeding bottle and the medicine bottle marked 'Spasmodic Mixture'.

Nursey took all three bottles to Home Office analyst Arthur Pearson Luff, who also lectured in medical jurisprudence at St Thomas's Hospital. At the same time, Nursey also gave the doctor the baby's nightdress and a sealed jar containing body parts, removed by doctors at her post mortem examination. Luff, who had not testified at the inquest, found acetic acid present in the vomit on the baby's clothing. The bottle belonging to Beatrice Clark, which was corked and sealed, contained just seven drops of strong acetic acid, considerably less than Beatrice remembered. Luff noted that the anti-spasmodic mixture was completely harmless, containing no noxious ingredients whatsoever. Meanwhile, an inspection of the excised portions of the baby's tongue, stomach and upper air passage showed that they appeared to have been eaten away by corrosive liquid.

Nursey also took statements from Mr and Mrs Myers and their servants after baby Ray's death. Once again, Emily gave conflicting accounts of her movements, first verbally, then in the written statement that she made for Mr Myers. Having read the written statement, Nursey brought Emily and Beatrice Clark together and asked Emily to repeat her assertion that she had seen Beatrice feeding Ray from a cup, which Beatrice denied vehemently. It was Nursey who eventually arrested and charged Emily Newber, who assured him 'I never, I never, I never done such a thing.'

Defence counsel Mr Booth was very concerned that Emily Newber could be suffering from symptoms relating to menstruation. He closely questioned the medical witnesses, who conceded that a girl aged between fourteen and fifteen '…would be very likely to be in a state of hysteria.' Joseph Bush added that this might produce 'hallucination and imagination' and that the statements of a person in such a state could not be relied upon to be truthful.

Female Warder   Emily Newber

However, when Dr Gimlet was recalled, he testified that, having examined Emily at the time of the poisoning, he had not seen '…the slightest trace of hysteria about her.' On the contrary, from her demeanour, Gimlet firmly believed that the nursemaid was suffering from homicidal mania. There was no evidence that Emily had ever menstruated, Gimlet informed the court, adding that this was the time during which hysteria often developed in young women. Questioned by Booth, the doctor stated that, whereas some girls began menstruating between the ages of thirteen and fourteen, many did not start until they were seventeen or eighteen years old.

With his defence largely negated by Gimlet, Booth could only remind the court that Emily had absolutely no motive whatsoever for murdering her charge and that, while alone in the house with the other children, she had plenty of opportunity to get rid of the poison bottle, while Mr and Mrs Myers and Beatrice Clark were with the doctor. Booth also suggested that, even if Emily did administer a poisonous substance to the baby, it was done without any intention of killing the infant but probably given in the hope of silencing its crying.

It took the jury only a few minutes' deliberation to find Emily Newber guilty of manslaughter, adding a recommendation for mercy on account of her age. Once the members of the jury had reached this conclusion, it was revealed that Emily had been sacked from several previous jobs on the grounds of cruelty to the children in her charge. Another employer had sacked her after she showed an unnatural interest in poisons kept on the premises.

In sentencing Emily Newber, Mr Justice Grantham commented that, in his opinion, she had been very properly convicted. In fact, the jury had taken a very compassionate view of her offence and would have been perfectly justified in convicting her of wilful murder. Taking the jury's recommendation for mercy into account, the judge announced his intention of passing a sentence that was in proportion to the prisoner's age. To that end, he sentenced Emily Newber to one week's imprisonment, followed by five years in a reformatory.

Emily sobbed bitterly as she was removed from court to begin her sentence. It is not known where she was incarcerated but records suggest that after her release, she went on to marry and have children of her own.

Note: There are numerous variations of names throughout the contemporary newspapers. Emily Newber is also referred to as Neuber, while Dr Gimlet is alternatively named Gimblet and Gibley. Although the name of the victim is written throughout as Ray, it is believed that this may be short for Rachel. Emily is also said to be both fourteen and fifteen years old. As always, I have used the most commonplace variant.

'I did it on purpose, as I want to do away with myself.'

Otley, Yorkshire, 1893.

Shortly before 8.00 p.m. 10 May 1893, a young man walked into the police station at Otley, Yorkshire, and calmly told PC Fearnside that he had come to give himself up, having killed his little brother with a chopper. 'I did it on purpose, as I want to do away with myself' stated sixteen-year-old Fred Cook, who was quickly locked up while the police went to investigate his claims.

When Superintendent Strain and PC Phillips reached Cook's home in Peel Crescent, the doors were locked and the house seemed deserted. Having gained entry, they found a toddler lying face down in a pool of blood on the kitchen floor, a bloody hatchet discarded at his side. Strain picked up the child, noticing a three-inch long wound on the upper part of the head, through which brain matter was protruding. The police sent for medical assistance but there was very little that Dr William Parker Pinder could do and, in spite of his best efforts, two-and-a-half-year-old Arthur Herbert Cook died at 10.35 p.m.

The following afternoon, coroner Mr T.P. Brown held an inquest at The Fleece Hotel, Otley. One of the first witnesses heard was Robert Cook, the father of both Arthur and Fred. Having identified Arthur's body, Mr Cook explained that, when he left the house at around 6.30 p.m., Fred and his mother were indoors, while Arthur was playing in the back yard with his other siblings. When Cook returned two hours later, it was to find Arthur mortally wounded on the kitchen table, being tended by his mother and three or four neighbours. Rebecca Cook told the inquest that she left the house at just before 7.00 p.m. to visit a doctor to get treatment for blood poisoning in her hand, leaving her children playing happily in the yard. When she returned ninety minutes later, Dr Pinder was in her kitchen, working desperately to try and save Arthur.

Mr and Mrs Cook insisted that Fred and Arthur were normally the best of friends and were very fond of each other. Both parents described Fred as a good boy, although they conceded that he had occasionally given them a bit of trouble by running away from home.

Having heard from Dr Pinder and the policemen, the coroner told the jury that, in his opinion, there was little doubt that Fred Cook had committed the act that caused the death of his little brother. Brown suggested that the jury should find a verdict of wilful murder against Cook and leave the judge and jury at the Assizes to ponder the important question of Fred's sanity. After ten minutes' deliberation, the jury did as he suggested.

In the wake of the inquest, numerous rumours about the murder began to circulate around Otley and, after reporting on the inquest, the *Yorkshire Evening Post* made an attempt to get to the truth of the matter. 'With regard to the mental condition of the accused, there is no doubt among those who knew him that he has lately been a bit queer' the newspaper reported, adding that Fred was known for his reticent, morose and sullen demeanour.

Neighbours suggested that Fred was inordinately fond of sensational literature, claiming that he read the so-called 'Penny Dreadfuls' by the dozen. It was also said that he was expected to do a lot of housework at home and had killed his brother by way of protest. Another explanation for the murder was that Fred was using the hatchet in the garden to build a rabbit hutch and lashed out when his little brother annoyed him.

The *Yorkshire Evening Post* set out to interview those who they believed could confirm or deny the rumours. The police felt it highly unlikely that Fred had reacted violently to something that his brother had done, given that he was so calm on his arrival at the police station.

'Did he seem at all sorry?' asked the reporter.

'Not particularly' replied the un-named police spokesperson. 'He did for a moment seem to cry a little but altogether he was comparatively calm.' Fred's demeanour on handing himself in was taken to demonstrate the unlikelihood that he had done a fearful deed in a temporary fit of passion, the police supposing instead that he had suddenly been seized with a homicidal mania. Asked how Cook was coping with being locked up, the interviewee stated that after the murder the boy '…slept as sound as a top' and ate a hearty breakfast of ham, eggs and coffee on waking. Taken from the cells at Otley Police Station to Armley Gaol, he was alternately bright, cheerful, chatty, morose and tearful.

Having spoken to the police, the reporter went to Fred's family, noting as he talked to Robert and Rebecca Cook that the body of their youngest son lay on a bed in the corner of the front room, covered by a small white sheet. The Cooks told the newspaper that Fred was a quiet, gentle boy who had never misbehaved himself in any way, apart from occasionally running away from home. Eleven weeks earlier, he had unexpectedly absented himself from his job as an apprentice in the printing machine making trade and was away for a week. He sent his parents a note to say that he was intending to make his way to the World's Fair in Chicago, although on the following day, the Cooks received another letter to say that he was on his way home.

Mrs Cook perpetually wrung her hands as she spoke to the journalist, repeating over and over again 'Oh, but he did love Arthur. He did love Arthur.' Robert Cook dispelled the rumours that Fred had been forced to do housework, emphasizing that his wife did all that was required in that department while Fred was at liberty to do pretty much as he pleased. As far as having to stay in at night and babysit his younger siblings, Mr and Mrs Cook insisted that they tried their hardest to persuade Fred to go out but he much preferred to stay at home and either read or play draughts.

Asked what Fred was reading at the moment, Rebecca Cook produced a pamphlet entitled 'The Golden Book of Health: A key to health, happiness and long life.' Having flicked through it, the *Yorkshire Evening Post* reporter opined 'The effects on such a temperament as the prisoner's of reading like this would not be likely to establish his sanity.'

The newspaper finished by talking to a fellow apprentice who worked with Fred, who revealed that Fred was a great fan of playing draughts during his lunch break. According to the unnamed youth, Fred worked well but in fits and starts – he was inclined to lose interest in tasks and then couldn't be persuaded to work at all. 'It was no use driving him if he made up his mind. He was a bit queer that way' explained the apprentice being interviewed. 'This statement quite harmonised with that made elsewhere by people who knew the prisoner even slightly' commented the reporter. 'It was admitted that his actions generally gave no indication of his mind being even in the slightest degree affected but it was equally admitted that there was something 'queer' – a latent spark of insanity perhaps – which might at some moment prove something dangerous.'

Committed for trial by both the coroner and later the magistrates, Fred Cook appeared before Mr Justice Bruce at Leeds Town Hall on 2 August 1893. He was defended by Mr Charles Mellor, while Mr Cyril Dodd Q.C. M.P. and Mr Kemp handled the prosecution for the Crown.

Dodd began by describing the events on the night of the murder, beginning with the defendant's arrival at Otley Police Station and leading on to the grim discovery made by the police when they went to Fred's home. By now, a new witness had emerged, who lived two doors away from the Cook family and worked with Fred as an apprentice at Messrs W. M. Dawson & Sons. Tom Walker stated that on the evening of the murder, Arthur was outside looking at some rabbits in a hutch when Fred called him to come into the house. Arthur didn't respond so Fred called again and, when he still wouldn't leave the rabbits, Fred walked outside, picked him up and carried him indoors. According to the prosecution, this indicated some degree of premeditation to murder, especially since the hatchet had been taken from its usual place in the cellar and the front door had been deliberately locked from the inside. However, when cross examined by the counsel for the defence, Walker was adamant that Fred did not sound as if he were angry with his brother.

Dr Pinder described being summoned to the house and finding Arthur on the kitchen table, a three-inch long, one-inch deep split in his skull, through which his brain protruded. Pinder stressed that Arthur's skull was quite thin and the chopper was very heavy. Its weight alone would have been sufficient to cause the fatal wound and, in the doctor's opinion, had any force been used, the wound would have been much deeper.

Fred, who was described as 'an intelligent-looking boy', listened intently to the witnesses, displaying very little emotion until his father was called to the witness box. As Robert Cook testified about Fred's good character and about the affection he always showed his brothers and sisters, Fred broke down and sobbed. Robert told the court that, as a young child, Fred had been overweight and bow legged and was consequently taunted by other children. Aged five, he had suffered from typhoid and nearly died.

Impression of Fred Cook in court (author's collection)

Robert Cook was followed into the witness box by Frank Armstead, who was in charge of Fred at Armley Gaol. Armstead stated that he had always found Fred to be intelligent and well behaved and that he showed no signs of mental aberration whilst in prison.

After the prosecution rested, defence counsel Mellor announced that he didn't intend to call any witnesses, leaving prosecuting counsel Dodd to begin his closing speech. Dodd maintained that Fred's motive for murder was his own wish to die and that, when he killed his brother, he knew exactly what he was doing and, in anticipating the gravest penalty of the law, fully understood that his actions were wrong.

Mr Mellor then addressed the jury for the defence, reminding them that Fred had hitherto borne an excellent character, was well behaved and conducted himself as a kindly elder brother. Yet the jury were being asked to believe that all of a sudden, without the slightest alteration in the atmosphere of peace and brotherly love that normally pervaded his family life, he took up a deadly weapon and, without any display of anger or violence, put an end to his brother's life. The evidence of motive was as feeble as the evidence of premeditation argued Mellor and there was not a tittle of evidence from which any suggestion of malice against the deceased could be drawn. Could this therefore have been an unintentional act, he asked?

Mellor suggested that having killed his brother unintentionally, carelessly and recklessly and knowing that nobody would ever believe that it was an accident, Fred had been so overcome with remorse that he wanted to die and had therefore decided to claim that Arthur's demise was by his own wilful act.

The law gave juries a merciful power, concluded Mellor, asking this jury to exercise their merciful discretion and say that it was a case of manslaughter. This well-disposed, affectionate and loving boy would have to pay the penalty of his act to his dying day and would always have the knowledge that he had killed the little brother he loved. This in itself was sufficient punishment, without adding the harsh measure of saying that it was a deliberate and wilful murder.

Mr Justice Bruce then summarised the case for the jury, reminding them that they simply had to determine whether they were satisfied that the prisoner committed the crime with the intention of killing his brother. The defence had suggested that Arthur's death was a tragic accident – perhaps the prisoner was playing with the hatchet and, by some dreadful mistake, it fell on his brother. This would not be murder. Yet, from the evidence of the police, doctors and prison warders, it could not be suggested that there was any derangement of mind and, as far as he could see, the prisoner knew what he was about. He had never claimed that Arthur's death was an accident – rather Fred had been quick to point out that he did it on purpose as he wanted to do away with himself. 'If you believe that he was recklessly playing with the hatchet, you may find any verdict which your consciences might enable you to find' concluded Bruce. ' If you think the prisoner was so confused in his mind that he did not know what he was about, you must disregard his statement to the police, however distinct that might be. But if you are satisfied that he did it on purpose then you cannot find any other verdict than guilty of wilful murder.'

The jury retired and, after an hour and twenty-five minutes, they returned to court to inform the judge that they were unable to reach an agreement. Mr Justice Bruce seemed perplexed, reiterating that the facts of the case were exceedingly simple and that all the jury had to decide was whether or not they believed the evidence that had been put before them. If they did, there was no doubt that the prisoner had killed his brother and said that he had done so on purpose, which would lead them to a verdict of guilty. If they did not believe the evidence, they must of course find the prisoner not guilty.

'One gentleman among us thinks he might have been insane for the moment' clarified the foreman of the jury.

'But there is no evidence whatsoever of that' argued Bruce. 'The prisoner has been ably represented and there was every opportunity to raise such a defence. Indeed, the Crown went almost out of its way to introduce medical witnesses, so that the question of insanity might easily have been raised if thought desirable'.

'The medical evidence does not apply to the time when the deed was committed' expanded one of the jurors.

'There is no evidence whatever of the prisoner being at any time irresponsible for his actions' insisted Bruce. It was perfectly true that no medical man examined the prisoner at the time and there could never be any doctor examining an accused person at the time he was committing the deed. It was a strong presumption in law that every person was responsible for his actions unless there was some irrefutable evidence to the contrary. In this particular case, there was no evidence of mental derangement either before or after the deed and, even if there were, it would not shield a person from the consequences of his crime unless it were such a derangement as to prevent him from knowing the character of his acts. With that, Bruce urged the jury to retire again to try and reach agreement.

It took just forty-five minutes for the jury to return, informing the judge that there was absolutely no possibility of them agreeing on a verdict and leaving Bruce with no option but to discharge them and order a retrial before a new jury.

The second trial took place on the following day and, on this occasion the jury returned after fifty minutes' deliberation with a guilty verdict, albeit with a very strong recommendation to mercy on account of the prisoner's tender age. Having assured the jury that he would forward their recommendation to the proper authorities, Bruce passed sentence of death. His words were accompanied by much sobbing from the crowded court room, although Cook himself remained perfectly cool. As he left the dock to be returned to Armley Gaol, he laughed and chatted with the warders and showed no concern for his fate. It was immediately announced that a petition was to be raised on his behalf for presentation to the Home Secretary and within days Cook appeared to have undergone a complete change of attitude, writing to his parents to say that he had placed his trust in God and would willingly die a thousand deaths to undo what he had done.

It was later announced that Cook had been reprieved and his sentence commuted to one imprisonment. He was released on licence in August 1900 but at the beginning of 1901, he was twice fined for being drunk and disorderly. In May 1901, he was sent to prison for three months for failing to report his whereabouts to the police, a condition of his licence. In 1902, he was charged with two counts of burglary in Nottingham and, as a result, his licence was revoked until July 1906, when he was again discharged. However, he persisted in leaving Otley without reporting his whereabouts to the police, travelling throughout both Yorkshire and Lancashire.

In March 1907, he was summoned to appear before magistrates at Otley to answer to a charge of failing to report a change of address. The Chairman of the Bench concluded that Cook was far too dangerous a character to be allowed at large without proper supervision and sentenced him to six months in prison.

It has not proved possible to establish what happened to Cook on his eventual release. However records suggest that he enlisted in the 9th Battalion of the East Yorkshire Regiment and died aged thirty-eight in October 1916.

'Where is your Ma?'

Plaistow, London, 1895.

On 5 July 1895, steamship steward Robert Coombes re-joined his ship *France*, leaving behind his wife of seventeen years, Emily Harrison Coombes and their two sons, Robert Allen and Nathaniel 'Natty' George, at their home at 35 Cave Road, Plaistow in East London. The following day, Emily's sister-in-law, (who was married to Robert's brother, Nathaniel, and was also named Emily Coombes) called to see her and the two women arranged to meet again on 8 July.

However, Robert's wife didn't turn up for their meeting and when her sister-in-law went to her house to see where she was, there was nobody at home. Emily went back several times but there was no response to her knocking until 15 July, when the door of the house in Cave Road was finally opened a crack by a man named John Fox, who was an acquaintance of Robert and Emily Coombes.

'Can I see Mrs Coombes?' asked Emily, to be told by Fox that she was not at home. When Emily pressed him for more information, Fox grudgingly revealed that Mrs Coombes was on holiday in Liverpool.

Emily didn't believe him and tried to force her way into the house but Fox was too strong for her and shut the door firmly in her face. As Emily reluctantly turned to leave, her nephews Robert and Natty appeared. Emily asked thirteen-year-old Robert where his mother was and he repeated Fox's explanation that she had gone to Liverpool, adding that an aunt had died there and left the family a lot of money and he was now very rich. While Emily tried to digest this information, Robert and Natty ran off with some other boys towards the recreation ground.

Now more concerned than ever, Emily returned to Cave Road with a neighbour but they were unable to gain entrance. They visited the missing woman's mother and a telegram was sent to Emily Harrison Coombes's aunt in Liverpool, to see if she was there. When a reply came back to say that she wasn't, Emily and the neighbour became even more determined to gain admittance to the house. On 17 July, they went to Cave Road several times and finally at 1.20 p.m. the door was opened by a strange man. Emily impatiently brushed him aside and once inside the house, she stormed into the back room where Fox, Robert junior and Natty were playing cards and smoking.

'Where is your Ma?' Emily asked Robert, who told her that his mother had gone to visit a neighbour and offered to take her there.

'Your Ma is in this house and I will not leave until the police arrive' argued Emily, at which point Natty scrambled out of the window and fled.

Emily grabbed Robert's arm and demanded to check his mother's bedroom.

'You can't. It's locked' Robert explained.

Emily went upstairs to see for herself and found that the bedroom door was indeed locked. Since Robert claimed not to know where the key was, Emily sent the neighbour to borrow a key from the landlady and the bedroom door was finally opened, releasing a waft of the foulest odour imaginable.

Emily Harrison Coombes lay on her back on the bed, dressed in blood-drenched nightclothes. She had apparently been dead for some time since her facial features, buttocks and calves had been almost entirely consumed by maggots. A post-mortem examination later confirmed the cause of her death as two stab wounds in her chest, both of which had pierced her heart. A blood stained knife that lay at the foot of the bed was obviously the murder weapon.

Having found her sister-in-law's body, Emily Coombes rounded on her nephew, calling him a bad, wicked boy, saying that he knew full well that his mother was dead and should have told the truth rather than lying and pretending she was still alive. Robert promised to tell his aunt what happened and revealed that, after their father went off to sea their mother had given Natty a good hiding for stealing food. According to Robert, Natty was terribly upset and threatened to kill her but later told his brother that he couldn't do it, asking Robert to kill her for him and promising to signal by coughing twice when Robert was to do the deed. Whenever their father was away, Robert slept in his mother's bed and, on the night of 7 July, she pushed him for wriggling too much and kicking his legs. Robert told his aunt that he got out of bed there and then and stabbed her twice. Leaving her to bleed to death, he covered her body and took Natty to Lords to watch a cricket match.

In the ten days between his mother's death and his aunt finding the body, Robert rifled his mother's purse, which contained £10 that his father had left her to pay all the bills while he was at sea. To avoid arousing suspicion, Robert used some of the money to pay the rent and also paid the tradesmen who delivered milk and groceries to the house. However, since he also freely treated his friends to ginger beer and ice cream, the money dwindled fast and Robert began to scheme to get more. On 10 July, he and Natty went to Victoria Dock in search of John Fox, who was a friend of his parents. Fox, who had occasionally gone to sea in the past, now did odd jobs and ran messages. He was described by the chief officer of the National Steamship Company as 'half-witted' and, since he normally slept wherever he could find a space to lay his head, he was more than willing when Robert asked him to go and stay at Cave Road with him and Natty, while their parents were 'away'.

Robert had plans for Fox, the first of which involved sending him to see the cashier at the National Steamship Company with a letter: 'Dear Sir,—Will you please advance the sum of £4, as my mother is very ill with Bright's disease and will have to pay a very heavy doctor's bill. Will you please bring it yourself or give it to John Fox. I remain yours truly, R. Coombes.'

Cashier John Hewson refused to release any money without seeing a doctor's certificate and four days later, Robert went into Hewson's office with a letter signed by a surgeon, which claimed that Emily Harrison Coombes was suffering from 'an internal complaint.'   Noting that the letter wasn't dated, Hewson refused to hand over any money and told Robert that he would come and see his mother himself. 'You will bring the money with you?' Robert asked him and Hewson promised that he would. However, since Robert had successfully conned £2 out of him two years earlier on a similar pretext, Hewson had no intention of visiting Mrs Coombes.

With that money making avenue closed to him, Robert next began to pawn his family belongings and, since he needed an adult to go to the pawn shop on his behalf, Fox was unwittingly set to work. Robert Coombes senior's gold plated watch and a silver plated watch belonging to Robert junior were pawned at one shop, a mandolin at another. The staff at both pawn shops later identified Fox as the person who had pledged the items for cash.

When the police searched the house at Cave Road, they found a letter that Robert had written to his father but not yet posted. 'Dear Pa,—I am very sorry to inform you that my Ma has hurt her hands, and that the sore on her finger has spread all over her hands, and is unable to write to you. Just before I wrote this letter a bill from Mr. Greenway has come in, so had to pay it. Please send her home a dollar or two; all very well, Ma's hand improving. We will ask £4 for the mocking-bird. I enclose the bill and receipt. Hoping you are well, I remain, your loving son, R. COOMBES'. In addition, there was a letter that Robert had written to a local newspaper, planning to take out a classified advertisement: '35, Cave Road, Barking Road. To the Evening News Office, 12, Whitefriars Street, Fleet Street, E.C., London:—"Sir,—Please be kind enough to place my advertisement in the Evening News. I enclose stamps. 'Wanted, £30 for six months. Will pay £6 a month for instalment.'

An inquest on Emily Harrison Coombes's death was opened on 19 July by West Ham coroner Mr C. C. Lewis and almost immediately adjourned. By the time it re-opened on 29 July, magistrates had already sat the Police Court in West Ham and charged both Robert and Natty with the wilful murder of their mother and John Fox with being an accessory after the fact. However, at the inquest, twelve-year-old Natty was called simply as a witness, the coroner painstakingly explaining to him that he need say nothing if he believed it would incriminate him.

Natty told the inquest that he usually attended Cave Road Board School but hadn't been since his father went to sea. Robert had left school in June of that year and got a job as a plater's helper but had quit his job after just two weeks and was yet to find another.

He recalled being given a thrashing by his mother the day after his father left but insisted that he had not suggested killing their mother to his brother and had never arranged to cough twice to signal when the killing should take place. Indeed, it had already been established that Robert had actually bought the knife with which he stabbed his mother from a shop in Barking Road at the beginning of July and had then hidden it at home, first in the dustbin and then up the chimney.

Natty believed that Robert had killed their mother so that he could go to India. He swore that the first he knew of the murder was when his brother woke him early on the morning of 8 July and said 'I have done it. I have killed her.'

'You ain't' Natty replied and Robert told him to come and see her if he didn't believe him. Natty got up and went to his mother's room. He stood quaking with fear in the doorway and, when his mother groaned, Natty fled back to his room and jumped into bed, pulling the covers over his head.

The brothers spent the next two days at Lords, watching cricket. Reluctant to go upstairs, they locked their mother's bedroom door and slept on a sofa and armchair in the back parlour until, on the third day, they decided to fetch Fox, who also slept downstairs on the floor.

Robert told Fox that their mother had gone to Liverpool and Fox didn't question what he was told. The three spent much of their time playing cricket in the street or playing cards. Fox was given some of the boys' father's clothes and, at Robert's urging, began to make plans to take the two boys to India.

The inquest was adjourned for a second time and when it was finally concluded on 1 August, the jury returned a verdict of wilful murder against Robert and a verdict of being an accessory before the fact on Nathaniel, who was promptly taken into custody.

In the event, both Robert and Nathaniel Coombes were tried at the Old Bailey for the wilful murder of their mother and John Fox with being an accessory after the fact. The proceedings were opened on 9 September 1895 by Mr Justice Kennedy and, when Robert was asked to plead, he immediately said 'Guilty'. On the advice of his counsel Mr Grantham, that plea was withdrawn and all three defendants then pleaded 'not guilty'.

Robert and Natty from the Illustrated Police News, 27 July 1895 (author's collection)

The judge first dealt with the charge against Nathaniel and when the prosecution declined to offer any evidence against him, Kennedy instructed the jury to acquit him, before turning his attention to Robert.

While confined in Holloway Prison prior to his trial, Robert seemed very excited by the prospect of appearing at The Old Bailey and now he was actually there, he amused himself by pulling grotesque faces and putting his tongue out at the judge. Since he had already made a full confession to the murder, the main task for the jury was to determine whether or not he was sane at the time.

Many of the witnesses at the trial knew Robert personally and were of the opinion that he was a bright boy, although with a tendency to be rude and cheeky at times. The headmaster of one school he had attended described him as 'a very clever boy for his age' but all of his former schoolmasters commented on his frequent long absences from school.

Robert's father described his son as 'excitable', informing the court that Robert's birth had been a difficult one and the boy still bore scars on his temples, made by the forceps used to deliver him. As far as Robert senior was aware, his oldest son was not delusional, although he did sometimes claim to hear noises in the house at night. Throughout his life, Robert junior suffered from headaches and fainting fits and he had been diagnosed with 'an affectation of the brain', which doctors labelled 'cerebral congenitis' (sic). His father had been warned never to chastise him by hitting his head and not to overtax his brain by giving him school work to do at home. Robert had also developed a fascination with the exploits of murderer James Canham Read, who shot his eighteen-year-old mistress near Southend in June 1894. According to his father, he even travelled by himself to Southend, saving up to pay his fare and then walking a considerable distance to catch a glimpse of the killer.

George Edward Walker, the medical officer at Holloway Prison, looked after Robert from 18 July until his trial. Walker had also seen the marks on Robert's head and noted that his head was misshapen and the pupils of his eyes were frequently different in size, all of which could be indicative of brain damage sustained during birth. Walker found Robert junior of weak intellect but, at times, highly excitable and, on one occasion, Robert had to be moved into a padded cell for five days for his own safety. He claimed to have heard voices urging him to 'Kill her, kill her, run away' and said that the reason he murdered his mother was because he was afraid that she would kill Natty if he did not. Much was made at the trial of Robert's choice of reading matter – he was a great fan of so-called 'penny dreadfuls' and the judge commented adversely on the lurid covers, which portrayed the contents as highly sensational and graphic.

While incarcerated, Robert showed no remorse for his actions, nor did he seem to appreciate the gravity of his situation, looking forward to his impending trial with glee and writing some very strange letters, which were produced in court. One included the lines: 'I think I will get hung, but I do not care as long as I get a good breakfast before they hang me. If they do not hang me I think I will commit suicide. That will do just as well. I will strangle myself. I hope you are all well. I go up on Monday to the Old Bailey to be tried. I hope you will be there I think they will sentence me to die. If they do I will call all the witnesses liars.—I remain, yours affectionately, R. A. Coombes'. Another letter contained a sketch of a scaffold with a hanging body and Robert had also written a mock will, in which he left various legacies amounting to thousands of pounds, including £300 to each of his prison warders.

Walker theorised that Robert suffered from intermittent attacks of homicidal mania and that he also experienced irresistible impulses. 'The boy's behaviour in prison and the absence of motive are unfavourable to sanity' concluded Walker, who was of the opinion that, when he killed his mother, Robert was unaware that what he was doing was wrong.

When the trial jury retired, they took just over an hour to agree that Robert Allen Coombes was guilty of the wilful murder, tempering their verdict with a recommendation of mercy. After a few words of advice from the judge, the jury retired again and, after two minutes, returned to clarify their verdict, finding Robert guilty but insane at the time of the crime.

Mr Justice Kennedy (author's collection)

Mr Justice Kennedy took a sympathetic view of the case against John Fox, suggesting to the jury that someone as devious as Robert could easily have hoodwinked a man with Fox's limited mental capacity. The jury concurred and were quick to pronounce Fox not guilty.

Robert Allen Coombes was ordered to be detained until her Majesty's pleasure be known and was taken back to Holloway Prison. He is believed to have been kept under close supervision for eighteen years before being released. Although it has proved impossible to establish what happened to him after his trial, there is anecdotal evidence that he left England for Australia in 1914, fighting with the A.M.C during the First World War and earning a military medal. It is believed that he died in Australia in 1945, aged sixty-five.

'He's stabbed me. Look at my arm.'

Accrington, Lancashire, 1896

Cabinet maker John Coates sold his furniture from premises on Warner Street, Accrington, and he and his wife Sarah lived above the shop, along with their son, Thomas. On 9 June 1896, John and Thomas were at their workshop, behind The Brown Cow public house in Bridge Street. Their fifteen-year-old apprentice of six months, Christopher Hindle, was sent on an errand, after which he was instructed to go back to the shop in Warner Street to clean and dust the furniture there.

Warner Street, Accrington (author's collection)

Christopher arrived in Warner Street at around 9.00 a.m., when sixty-one-year-old Sarah Coates was alone upstairs, doing the ironing. At around 10.15 a.m., Christopher appeared at his employer's workshop and breathlessly told John and his son that Mrs Coates had been murdered.

'Nonsense! Nothing of the sort.' replied John but Christopher was insistent.

'Yes, she has, by a strange man.' The apprentice held out his arm. 'He's stabbed me. Look at my arm.' Seeing that Christopher did indeed appear to be bleeding, John and Thomas rushed home, where they found Sarah lying on the bedroom floor, blood gushing from a wound in her throat. Her false teeth had fallen from her mouth and lay in a puddle of blood, along with threepence in copper coins. Thomas sent Christopher for a doctor and asked a neighbour to go for the police, before wrapping wet towels around his mother's neck to try and staunch the bleeding. Even so, when Dr Clayton arrived only minutes later, the injured woman's blood had spread across the bedroom floor and was beginning to trickle down the stairs.

Clayton removed the blood-drenched towels and found a three-and-a-half-inch long wound on the right side of her neck. Mrs Coates was semi-conscious; she groaned repeatedly and, when questioned about who had done this to her she responded 'Nobody', before asking to be turned over. Her face was discoloured and the doctor surmised that she had been strangled as well as cut, his conclusions confirmed by the presence of bruising around her throat. A scarf was loosely knotted around her neck, which Clayton suspected had been pulled tight and twisted. Dr Monaghan arrived minutes after Clayton but the two doctors were unable to save the injured woman, who died within minutes. A post mortem examination carried out by police surgeon Dr Geddie confirmed Clayton's suspicions. Attempts had been made to strangle Sarah Coates, both manually and with her silk scarf but the cause of death was loss of blood from the cut on her neck.

Police officers were very quickly on the scene. PC Andrews was patrolling his beat at the end of Church Street, when a man rushed up to him and told him 'There's been some throat cutting up here at the top end of Warner Street'. Police Sergeant Bale was alerted to Sarah's plight by Christopher Hindle, as he returned from fetching the doctor. Naturally, since Christopher had been alone in the house with his employer's wife, the officers were very interested in hearing his account of what had happened to cause her death.

Christopher told the police that he was dusting in the shop when he heard a piercing scream from upstairs. He immediately went to investigate and found Mrs Coates struggling on the floor with a man, who was trying to strangle her. As Christopher entered the room, the man pulled out a knife and cut her throat. Christopher stated that he had grabbed the intruder's coat tails and tried to pull him away from Mrs Coates but the man slashed at him with the knife, cutting his arm several times and forcing Christopher to let go. The man then ran downstairs, through the store room and into the back yard, where he scrambled over the wall. Christopher followed but lost him a couple of streets away, after which he went to the workshop to alert Mr Coates and Thomas to the tragedy.

According to Christopher, the murderer was between twenty-eight and thirty years old and stood around 5'8" tall. He had a dark complexion with a black moustache and was smartly dressed in a navy blue suit, with a fashionable low-cut waistcoat, a blue tie and a dark brown cap. Based on this very detailed description, the police began a search for Mrs Coates's killer, alerting staff at the station and also contacting their colleagues in neighbouring towns to be on the lookout.

Yet, although they were actively searching for the suspect, some officers had suspicions about the truth of Christopher's account of Mrs Coates's last minutes. Having done all he could for the dying woman, Dr Clayton turned his attention to dressing the seventeen wounds on Christopher's arms. Clayton then spoke to the police, pointing out that all but two of the cuts were little more than 'chicken scratches' and that all were located on the inside of the right arm. The knife cuts were also nearly parallel and thus, in Clayton's opinion, were unlikely to be the work of a crazed knifeman lashing out at random for five minutes but were almost undoubtedly self-inflicted. Not only that but the bedroom in which Mrs Coates was killed showed no signs that a life and death struggle had taken place between Hindle and her killer.

The murder weapon found lying near to Mrs Coates, was a pocket knife owned by her son, which he had left on a shelf in his bedroom. The knife was practically unique, since it had a highly unusual mechanism to open and close it. Thomas was adamant that the knife had been left closed and was confident that only he, his parents, or someone closely associated with the house would be able to figure out how to open it.

Christopher had stated that the murderer escaped by climbing over a wall surrounding the property's back yard. The wall was nine feet high and was topped by spikes, making it a very difficult climb, although it was possible for someone to use the yard gate to assist himself in scrambling up the wall, as Christopher himself claimed to have done. Yet there were no marks whatsoever on the gate and, considering that Christopher was bleeding, neither were there any spots of blood. Throughout the morning of the murder, two workmen were working at the rear of the shop. They were positioned on scaffolding, which gave them a clear view into the back yards. Both men were positive that nobody had exited the Coates's premises and that they had seen nobody at all in the back yards, apart from a woman hanging out washing at number 6 Warner Street. That woman was Mrs Rebecca Franks, who corroborated the story of the two labourers, stating that she had hung her washing out at around 9.30 a.m., after which she sat outside on a chair. She had a clear view of the back of the Coates's shop and swore that nobody had left the premises that way. Furthermore, neither the labourers nor Mrs Franks had heard any cries for help, even though Christopher claimed to have shouted out 'Murder! Stop that man!' as he passed them in pursuit of the killer.

An inquest was opened at Accrington Borough Police Court by coroner Mr H. J. Robinson. Local solicitor Mr Withers attended on behalf of Hindle and challenged some of the witnesses as they gave their testimony. Mrs Sarah Eidsforth stated that she had heard Hindle run out of the front door of the shop, slamming it behind him and disappearing down the passage at the side of the property. She had next seen him approaching the shop minutes later, accompanied by two policemen. Withers challenged Mrs Eidsforth, forcing her to concede that had the door not slammed, she would not have noticed Hindle leaving. Mrs Ellen Bradley told the inquest that she had a clear view of the rear of the Coates's property from her kitchen and that, on the morning of the murder, nobody had entered or left the yard. However, Withers forced an admission that Mrs Bradley had very briefly left her viewpoint at the kitchen sink, although she insisted that she would still have been able to hear anyone at the rear of her neighbour's property.

Workman William Wilkinson described his position on the scaffolding and consequent clear view of the back yard. Wilkinson was unshakeable in his insistence that nobody left the yard, as was his labourer, Alexander Forrrest, although the latter did admit that there were times when he was working a few yards away from Wilkinson, thus his view was sometimes obscured.

Both John and Thomas Coates swore that money had been missed from the house on several occasions, as recently as the day before the murder, when Thomas claimed that eight shillings had vanished from a drawer.

The inquest then heard from three medical witnesses, Dr Clayton, Dr Monaghan and police surgeon Dr Geddie. Clayton and Monaghan, who had been summoned to Warner Street, gave almost identical testimonies, agreeing that it was impossible for Mrs Coates to have cut her own throat. Both doctors believed that her assailant was 'a tolerably strong person', since Mrs Coates was robust and vigorous for her age.

Dr Geddie described his post mortem examination on the victim and related that he had found bruising on her left temple, as well as marks on her neck suggesting that she had been gripped tightly by a hand. There were several small abrasions, which Geddie believed to have been caused by the killer's fingernails digging in to the skin on the elderly woman's throat. In addition, there were further marks, which had been made by something being pulled tightly around her neck from behind. Geddie reiterated that the cause of death was haemorrhage from the cut throat, which had severed Mrs Coates's jugular vein.

It was left to the coroner to summarise the evidence for the jury, which he did at length. He advised them to start by considering whether or not Mrs Coates came to her death by violence against her and, if so, was there *prima facie* evidence against any one person in particular. The jury had heard the facts of the case from various witnesses and had also heard the statement made by Christopher Hindle. Was there anything that might lead the jury to suppose that Hindle had played a part in Mrs Coates's demise?

As far as the coroner could see, the jury had little option other than to return a verdict of wilful murder, since Mrs Coates couldn't possibly have taken her own life, therefore it stood to reason that somebody else must have taken it. If the jury believed that this somebody was Hindle, they must say so, to allow the case to be heard through the proper legal channels.

The jury debated for more than an hour before returning with their verdict – Mrs Coates had been murdered and there was *prima facie* evidence against Christopher Hindle, who was immediately arrested and taken into custody. After appearing before magistrates, it was reported that Christopher showed no signs of anxiety at his situation, laughing and joking with the guards outside his cell in Preston Gaol.

Christopher appeared before Mr Justice Cave at the Lancaster Assizes on 8 July 1896, when he was described by the contemporary newspapers as '…the most collected person in court', his composure only faltering towards the end of the trial, when his mother entered the witness box to speak about her son's character.

Mr Justice Cave (author's collection)

Mr McKeand and Mr Ambrose Jones opened the case for the prosecution by describing the morning of 9 June, referring to Christopher's version of events as '…improbable, even impossible.' A few days after the murder, a policeman had discovered twenty-five shillings and sixpence hidden under the front window of the shop, with a few spots of blood nearby. The victim was known to have some money in the house that she had collected for charity and it was supposed that Hindle had stolen then concealed the cash, planning to retrieve it when the heat had died down.

After hearing from those witnesses who had already spoken at the inquest, Mr Shee Q.C. spoke in defence of Hindle. He reminded the jury that the boy's mother had described him as an honest, kindly, straightforward boy and the most affectionate of all her children. The prosecution had devoted themselves almost entirely to proving that this boy had told a lie. 'Of course he told a lie' sneered Shee. Boys did tell lies. It was one thing to prove that someone had told a lie but another thing entirely to prove that he committed a murder.

The prosecution had tried to prove that the murderer had not climbed over the back wall. Well, maybe he hadn't. There were plenty of places in which he could have concealed himself, including three open ash pits and Hindle could just have assumed that the man had climbed the wall and escaped. Shee pointed out that there was no blood on the coins hidden beneath the shop window sill, nor was there any blood on Hindle, other than that which might have come from the cuts on his arms. Given that Mrs Coates's jugular vein had been severed, Shee felt that this was somewhat surprising.

The medical evidence suggested that Mrs Coates was initially strangled from the front, meaning that she would have seen her killer. When asked by the police who had done this to her, she could only say 'Nobody'. Surely it would have been just as easy to say 'Hindle' or 'Christopher' or even 'the boy'? Shee suggested that 'Nobody' might mean '…nobody that the victim knew or could identify'.

Mr Justice Cave then summed up the evidence for the jury, admitting that it was theoretically possible for an unknown man to have found his way into the house that morning. However, according to Hindle, this stranger was far too smartly dressed to be an ordinary tramp and the deceased was not known to have an enemy in the world, particularly one who would seek to murder her.

The stranger could not have got into the house through the back, as the door was barred and, if he had entered the premises from the front, he would have had to pass Hindle, who was there dusting. The judge asked the jury why Hindle grabbed the man by the coat tails instead of running for help and shouting 'Murder!' Neighbours and people in the streets had heard no such cries. There was also the matter of the injuries to Hindle's arm that were far too insignificant and regular to have been caused by a man wildly striking out with a knife. Finally, the judge pointed out that it was unlikely that a stranger would have concealed the money where it was found, since he would have no way of entering the house to recover it.

The jury retired for twelve minutes before returning with a guilty verdict, adding that they wished to recommend the prisoner to mercy on account of his youth. Hindle listened impassively as Mr Justice Cave passed the mandatory death sentence, before leaving for Lancaster Castle and later Strangeways Prison in Manchester.

On 28 July 1896, the mangled body of a man named Murray was found on the railway line near Brent Bridge, Leyland. It was claimed that Murray had been drinking heavily of late and that he had committed suicide because he was feeling remorseful, having committed a murder in Accrington. Drink had loosened Murray's tongue to the extent that he talked almost constantly about what he had done. His physical appearance closely matched Hindle's description of the murderer and many people believed that his account matched the boy's story - indeed Hindle himself wrote to his father from prison, telling him 'I'm on the track of the real culprit.' However, after Murray's apparent suicide a man named Joseph Iddon came forward, saying that he had met Murray, while he was walking to Accrington to hand himself in. Iddon claimed that

Murray had categorically denied having been involved in 'the Hindle affair', insisting that the murder he was suspected of having committed was of a woman and two children.

Portland Convict Prison (author's collection)

Within two weeks of the trial, Hindle's death sentence was commuted to one of life imprisonment and he was eventually sent to Portland Convict Prison in Dorset. In 1910, he is believed to have gone to Canada, returning to England to enlist in the Royal Engineers in February 1916. He is thought to have died in 1957.

Note: Mrs Eidsforth is also named Edisforth in contemporary accounts of the murder. However records suggest that her name may actually have been Edsforth. Dr Geddie's name is alternatively spelled Geddy in some reports.

'Another boy has taken Freddy away.'

Stockton-On-Tees, County Durham, 1903.

Saturday 30 May 1903 was a sunny day and, in the afternoon, Harold Hughes of Bickersteth Street, Stockton-On-Tees was sent out to play with his fifteen-month-old brother, Frederick. A short while later, Harold was brought home by a little girl. Between sobs, the distraught child told his mother 'Another boy has taken Freddy away', explaining that an older boy had taken his brother off to get some sweets.

Concerned neighbours and the police began an immediate search for the missing toddler, while Harold's mother Georgina quizzed him for more details. The three-year-old told her that Freddy had been taken by a boy who was selling newspapers on the street, who he described as barefoot and having one eye larger than the other.

The frantic search for Freddy ended the following morning, when two young boys named Ernest Harris and Frederick Joynes contacted the police, having spotted a baby's leg and elbow protruding from waste ground on the site of the old West Stockton Iron Works. An inquest on Freddy's death was opened on 1 June. By that time, police had traced a barefoot boy named Ferguson, who sold newspapers. Although Ferguson admitted to having been in the area at the relevant time, he denied having seen either Harold or Freddie. However, he then gave a statement to the police, in which he claimed to have seen a man cutting Freddie's throat and then burying him at the Iron Works.

Since a post-mortem examination showed no evidence of any attempt to cut Freddy's throat, it was obvious that Ferguson wasn't being truthful and, when challenged by the police, he admitted that he was telling lies. Nevertheless, the coroner asked Freddy's mother to place Harold in front of Ferguson and another boy of a similar age and stature. When Harold was then asked if he could see the boy who had taken his brother, he pointed first to Ferguson, then to the other boy. With no conclusive evidence to connect Ferguson to Freddy, the inquest jury eventually returned a verdict of wilful murder by person or persons unknown.

Meanwhile, the police continued their investigations pronouncing themselves baffled. Whoever had abducted Freddy must have taken him along the High Street, which would have been teeming with people, since a busy market was being held at the time. In addition, the toddler was buried in open ground that was not only accessible to the public but was also overlooked by numerous houses, not to mention the busy platform of the local railway station.

On 7 June 1903, Tommy Lynes of Stockton-On-Tees was wheeling his nineteen-month-old sister Fanny around in a makeshift perambulator, made from a soap box mounted on wheels. Near to the railway station, Tommy left his sister for a few minutes but when he returned she had gone. Looking round, Tommy spotted a bigger boy pushing the perambulator in the direction of Newtown, where the West Stockton Iron Works was located. Tommy ran home to his mother, who chased after the cart containing her daughter. She caught up with the perambulator as it crossed some waste ground and rescued her child. Aware that little Freddy had been found dead in that area only days earlier, Eliza Lynes took a firm grasp of the arm of the boy who had stolen her daughter and insisted that he accompany her home. There, to her astonishment, the boy confessed that he had intended to drown baby Fanny, at which he was promptly handed over to the police.

When questioned by Inspector Yeandle, the boy gave his name as Patrick Knowles, (a.k.a. O'Brien). Patrick claimed to be ten years old; although it would later emerge that he was actually only eight. He freely admitted to having taken Freddy, who he said was standing alone in the street crying. According to Patrick, he carried the child some way along High Street before setting him down and continuing until Freddy was too tired to walk any further. When Patrick picked him up again, Freddy went to sleep in his arms, not waking until Patrick placed him on his back in a shallow hollow that he had scooped in the loose earth at the disused Iron Works. Freddy immediately began to cry for his mother, so Patrick pulled the toddler's pinafore over his face, before covering him with soil and stones and going home. Over the next few days he told two of his friends what he had done.

High Street, Stockton-On-Tees (author's collection)

Once Patrick had confessed to murdering Freddy, the police were able to find other evidence to support his confession and he was charged and taken before magistrates at Stockton Police Court, where he was initially seated next to a woman who was charged with drunkenness. When her case had been heard, Patrick was moved to a bench in the body of the court, where he sat stoically as the clerk read out the charge that he had '…on 30 May, feloniously, wilfully and with malice aforethought, killed and murdered one Frederick

Hughes, a fifteen-month-old baby, against the peace of our Sovereign Lord and King, his Crown and dignity.' Dressed in blue trousers and a ragged corduroy jacket, Patrick seemed completely unmoved by his predicament, gazing around the court room and fiddling with his cap, which lay on his lap. Told that he might make a statement, he remained silent, not even speaking to acknowledge his younger sister when she evaded their parents' clutches and scrambled onto the bench next to her brother.

Solicitor Mr T. W. Malkin, who had been appointed to represent Patrick, advanced the theory that Patrick may have taken baby Freddy with the intention of acting kindly towards him. Perhaps he had given him food, which had sent the baby into convulsions, causing Patrick to panic and bury him, argued Malkin. However the magistrates were not convinced and committed Patrick for trial at the next Durham Assizes, to be held on 14 July. He left the police court seemingly unconcerned, singing comic songs as he was taken to Durham Gaol to await his trial.

While in prison, Patrick was examined by doctors and found to be 'mentally deficient', the doctors stating that, while he was neither '…imbecile nor lunatic', from a medical point of view he should be regarded as 'constructively insane'. Questioned about his motives for killing, all Patrick could say was that it was fun to hear the baby crying. On receiving this diagnosis, the Home Secretary ordered that he should not face trial but instead be moved to Broadmoor Criminal Lunatic Asylum with immediate effect. It was later reported that Patrick had buried another toddler in March 1903, although fortunately that child was rescued alive, after its screams were heard by a man as he walked past its intended grave.

Because of his age, Patrick was not sent directly to Broadmoor but was instead moved from Durham Prison to Cannington Industrial School at Westbury on Trym, near Bristol. However, almost immediately his identity was accidentally revealed, making it impossible for him to stay there. Thus in August 1903, he was sent on license from Broadmoor to St Thomas' Home Industrial School in Preston, where he remained until he was sixteen and was transferred back to Broadmoor, where he was trained as a tailor. A year later, he was again sent out on licence, this time to the Tulketh Auxiliary Home in Preston, where he remained until his discharge and release from Broadmoor in 1912. At that time, it was said that he was contemplating emigrating to Australia but it has proved impossible to verify whether or not he actually went.

'There has been a little upset at home.'

Meldreth, Cambridgeshire, 1904.

Shortly before 9.00 p.m. on 12 April 1904, fifteen-year-old Frank Rodgers appeared at The British Queen public house in Meldreth, Cambridgeshire, carrying his six-year-old sister in his arms. 'Would you mind looking after Queenie for the night?' Frank asked landlady Charlotte Elizabeth Thurley, explaining 'There has been a little upset at home.'

Mrs Hurley asked what had happened and was shocked when Frank calmly replied 'I have shot mother.' Thinking that there had possibly been some sort of minor accident with a toy pistol, Mrs Hurley pressed him for more details.

'I have shot mother' repeated Frank. 'Don't worry, it will be all right. I shall go to Melbourn [to the nearest police station] tomorrow'. Leaving his sister safe with Mrs Thurley he then headed back to his family's home, The Gables, which was located opposite the public house.

The Gables, Meldreth (author's collection)

Mrs Thurley hurriedly put Queenie into bed with her own daughter then followed him a few minutes later, finding Frank standing in the road outside his home.

'Is there anything I can do?' she asked and Frank suggested that she went into the house, claiming that his family's servants were afraid.

When Mrs Thurley went indoors Dr Octavius Robert Ennion was already in attendance, having been fetched by Frank's older sister, Winifred. On first arriving at the house, Ennion spoke to Frank, who was then in the kitchen.

'I've done it' Frank remarked to Ennion, pointing towards the hall, where forty-two-year-old Georgina Rodgers was slumped on the floor, her head and right arm resting on a sofa. Ennion immediately noticed that Georgina reeked of alcohol and a brief examination confirmed that she was dead from a single gunshot, the bullet having penetrated the left side of her neck roughly an inch below her ear, severing her jugular veins and carotid arteries, before exiting approximately two inches below her right ear.

Realising that he could do nothing to help Mrs Rodgers, Ennion went back to the kitchen and asked Frank for the gun, which the youth took out of his coat pocket and handed to the doctor.

'Did she suffer any pain?' Frank asked Dr Ennion and was reassured that his mother had most probably died within seconds of being shot. Suggesting that Frank should return to The British Queen, Ennion then went to the police station at Melbourn, arriving there at 9.15 p.m. He handed over the weapon to PS Charles Salmon, who accompanied him back to The Gables.

Meldreth, 1916, showing The British Queen on the left (author's collection)

Having viewed the body of Mrs Rodgers, Ennion and Salmon crossed the road to the pub, where Frank was sitting calmly reading a newspaper. He was arrested and charged with causing the death of his mother by shooting and taken to Melbourn Police Station to await the inquest and an appearance before magistrates. The inquest was scheduled for 13 April but, at the request of Frank's father, the coroner agreed to adjourn it for twenty-four hours so that legal representation could be arranged for Frank. Thus, on 14 April, Frank appeared before magistrates at Melbourn Police Court, where he was remanded for one week.

Later that day, he was taken back to The British Queen, where an inquest was opened by coroner Mr A. J. Lyon. Once the jury had viewed the body, Frank's father, William Alexander Rodgers was the first to testify, identifying the dead woman as his wife. Mr Rodgers was a London solicitor, who had moved his family to Meldreth a year or so before the shooting. He spent much of his time in London, visiting his wife and children at weekends. Two sons, Robert and Henry, were away at boarding school but twenty-one-year-old William and eighteen-year-old Winifred still lived at home with their mother, as did Frank and their youngest sister, Georgina Marian Roberts, known to everyone as 'Queenie'.

The inquest was told that on the night of the shooting, William junior was out, while his father was staying in London. The other members of the Rodgers family ate supper together, after which Frank went upstairs and Winifred went into the drawing room, where she began to play the piano, leaving their mother sitting in an armchair in what was known as the breakfast room. After ten minutes, Frank walked into the drawing room and announced to Winifred that he had shot their mother. 'I think it's for the best' he declared.

Frank Rodgers (1904) Author's collection.

In disbelief, Winifred rose to go to their mother but Frank prevented her, saying that someone had better go and fetch a doctor. After arguing briefly with Frank over which of them should go for Dr Ennion, Winifred eventually went with one of the servants, while Frank carried Queenie across the road to the safety of the pub.

Winifred testified at the inquest that, because she was playing the piano, she had not actually heard the shot that killed her mother and thus the first she knew of the shooting was when her brother walked into the drawing room carrying a revolver in his right hand. She later asked Frank why he had shot their mother and he replied 'I did it for Queenie's sake; she could not be brought up to the life we have led the last few years.'

Asked by the coroner if she understood what her brother meant by this remark, Winifred revealed that for the past few years their mother had 'given way to drink', making the whole family unhappy.

Winifred assured the inquest that there was no quarrel between her brother and her mother that evening. The family had eaten supper together, although Mrs Rodgers had barely touched her food but concentrated on drinking and, after supper, she sat in an armchair near the fireplace and dozed. According to Winifred, Georgina Rodgers had never ill-treated any of her children and had been especially close to Frank, who was apparently her favourite child. Frank was so close to his mother that his siblings called him 'Mother's Boy' and Winifred stated that he seemed particularly depressed whenever their mother was under the influence of alcohol.

Having been the Rodgers's family doctor since they moved to Meldreth, Dr Ennion corroborated much of Winifred's evidence. He began by describing his visit to The Gables in the immediate aftermath of the shooting then detailed the post-mortem examination that he had carried out on Georgina Rodgers on the day after her death. He confirmed the cause of her death as haemorrhage resulting from a single shot to the neck, assuring the jury that, given the location of the wound it was highly improbable that dead woman had shot herself. Ennion was then asked about his dealings with the Rodgers family before the tragedy.

The doctor told the inquest that Mrs Rodgers was frequently under the influence of drink. He estimated that he had seen her about forty times since the Rodgers family moved to Meldreth and on each occasion she was either drunk or recovering from the effects of excessive drinking. Ennion had also been caring for Frank, who had recently undergone a very rapid growth spurt and, for the six weeks prior to the shooting, had suffered from violent headaches and nosebleeds, which occurred almost every morning.

As he had done since the shooting, Frank Rodgers showed very little emotion, listening impassively to the evidence given at the inquest and both Sergeant Salmon and Dr Ennion were of the opinion that he had so far failed to comprehend the gravity of his position. Ennion told the inquest that he had seen Frank on the day after the murder, at which time Frank said that he had felt a sudden impulse to kill his mother. Immediately after supper, he went to his brother's bedroom, where he knew that William kept a revolver and bullets in a drawer. Frank described battling for some time to resist the uncontrollable urge to shoot his mother but told the doctor that he had suddenly felt very dizzy and heard voices urging him to 'Do it quickly'. Ennion also told the inquest that for some months, Frank had continually felt that his mother was standing behind him and, when he looked over his shoulder, he believed that he caught a brief glimpse of her, before she disappeared from view.

Ennion concluded his evidence at the inquest by informing the coroner that there was a history of insanity in the Rodgers family. One of Frank's uncles was confined in an asylum and a great uncle had died of epilepsy in an asylum in Australia. In addition, Mrs Rodgers's father was said to be addicted to intemperance and Ennion told the inquest that these revelations might have a bearing on Frank's legal responsibility for the shooting.

One of the final witnesses to testify at the inquest was Frank's older brother, William. Having admitted to owning the gun, William stated that he had been out at the time of the shooting and had returned home at about 9.00 p.m. to find his mother dead.

William crossed the road to The British Queen, where Frank was sitting reading the newspaper. 'Frank, do you know what you have done?' William asked his brother.

'I did it for Queenie's sake' Frank explained.

'But do you really know what you have done?' William asked.

'Oh, don't worry me' Frank replied dismissively.

Artist's impression of Frank Rodgers, (1904). Author's collection.

William outlined some changes in his brother's behaviour over the past few weeks, explaining that Frank had been unusually quiet and irritable for some time. He was very restless while sleeping and often got up in the middle of the night to lock the doors. Previously interested in gardening and in learning shorthand, Frank lost all interest in these pastimes and, according to William, hung around the house doing nothing, unable to settle his mind to anything. About three weeks before the shooting Mrs Rodgers had been particularly drunk and Frank disclosed at breakfast the following day that he had dreamed that he had strangled their mother. Finally William told the inquest that, in January 1904, Frank had risked his own life to save his mother from being knocked down by a train at a level crossing.

After hearing evidence from pub landlady Charlotte Thurley, the coroner summarised the evidence, telling the jury that, having heard what had been said, he believed the jury could only conclude that the cause of death was a bullet wound, resulting from a gun being fired at the deceased by Frank Rodgers. If the jury came to that conclusion, the coroner reminded them that the law presumed that all cases of homicide were murder, unless specific evidence was given to the contrary. Since there had been no such evidence submitted, coroner Mr Lyon suggested that the only possible verdict was that the deceased was wilfully murdered by her son.

The vicar of Meldreth, Reverend Percy Harvey, who was serving on the coroner's jury, asked if Winifred Rodgers's statement might be read to them and the coroner obliged. The jury then asked to further question Dr Ennion to rule out any possibility that the fatal gunshot wound was self-inflicted. Ennion was adamant that, although he could not say that it was completely impossible for Mrs Rodgers to have shot herself, there was no blackening around the wound caused by gunpowder, suggesting that the barrel of the gun had been more than two feet away when the shot was fired. Not only that but the wound was located on the left-hand side of Mrs Rodgers's neck and she was known to be right handed.

The jury discussed the case for around fifteen minutes before returning to say that they had reached a unanimous verdict that the deceased Georgina Rodgers died on 12 April from injuries received from a bullet discharged at her from a revolver by Frank Rodgers.

'That is a verdict of wilful murder' clarified the coroner, committing Frank for trial at the Cambridge Assizes.

Frank Rodgers was housed in the county gaol, Cambridge, until 3 June 1904, when he appeared before Mr Justice Phillimore at the Cambridge Assizes. Although he was said to be 'pale and trembling' he showed no signs of emotion, sitting in the dock with his head bowed as the case against him unfolded.

Mr H. St John Raikes opened for the prosecution, reminding the court that the circumstances of the case were especially sad because the victim was the mother of the prisoner. Given that he was the prosecuting counsel rather than the defence, Raikes then rather charitably pointed out that Mrs Rodgers was '…strongly addicted to the use of liquor' and seeing his mother in a drunken state distressed Frank and caused him a great deal of grief.

Winifred and William Rodgers both described the apparent transformation in their brother's personality in the weeks prior to the shooting, noting that he had changed from being an affectionate, good-tempered boy to a morose and irritable young man, who was unable to sleep or to concentrate on even the most menial tasks. They both stated that Frank had shown a particular interest in reading about Ernest Walton Lee in the newspapers. After a quarrel, fifteen-year-old Lee from Small Heath in Birmingham fatally stabbed his mother with a sharpened file. Only a couple of days before the shooting of Mrs Rodgers, it was reported that an inquest jury had determined that Mrs Walton was struck in the heat of passion, finding a verdict of manslaughter against Lee, who was said to have been very good to his mother.

Dr Ennion then described his findings on arriving at the scene of the shooting and the conclusions he drew from his post-mortem examination on Mrs Rodgers. Under cross examination from defence counsel Mr F. Low K.C., Ennion testified that he had seen the victim under the influence of alcohol at least forty times in the year preceding her death. He also described being called to attend Frank, who was suffering from violent headaches and nosebleeds. The doctor ventured an opinion that Frank had behaved in a most unnatural way after the shooting. He had talked about school and didn't seem to realise that he had done anything wrong and Ennion believed that the constant stress and strain of seeing his beloved mother intoxicated had so upset Frank's nervous system that he was under the impression that he was actually justified in shooting her.

Mr Justice Phillimore, author's collection.

The prosecution then called Charlotte Thurley, PS Salmon and Superintendent Wilderspin before resting their case and giving way to the defence. Mr Low began by calling Dr Robert Percy Smith, who claimed to have made an extensive study of mental illness. Smith had examined Frank on 18 April and told the court that he believed that the deceased woman's family had a history of mental disorder, which, in his opinion, prevented Frank from making a sound, rational judgement at the time he committed the shooting. Smith's opinion was supported by a London specialist in mental disorders, Dr A. C. Bastian and also by Dr E. Coulton Rogers, the

Medical Superintendent at the Cambridgeshire Asylum. Having examined Frank, Coulton Rogers formed the opinion that, at the time of the commission of the shooting, Frank was in a state of 'morbid mental exaltation' and although he made some effort to resist, he finally yielded to a recurrent impulse to commit a crime '…for which an immature judgement had for some time led him to believe there was moral justification.'

Low then called upon several of Frank's family members to give evidence of the family history of intemperance and mental disorders.

It then fell to Low to sum up the case for the defence. Referring to Frank as 'the boy' throughout his speech, he asked the jury to consider whether he was criminally responsible for the death of his mother or whether his mind was in such a state that, at the very outset of his adult life, they would be forced to conclude that he must bear the stain and disability of lunacy? There was no disputing the fact that the mother of this boy perished by his hand, although it was questionable whether the boy's mind was acting in conjunction with that hand. It was hardly possible that a boy who lived with his mother on such terms of affection could wilfully and maliciously have terminated her life argued Low, before concluding that, by reason of mental disease, the boy was not amenable to the ordinary laws and was therefore not guilty.

Prosecuting counsel Mr Raikes protested that all of the medical specialists called by the defence had failed to show conclusively that the prisoner was suffering from any definite form of mental disease but the jury found Frank Rodgers guilty but insane and he was ordered to be detained during the King's pleasure. He was sent to Broadmoor Criminal Lunatic Asylum.

Reports from Broadmoor show that he was 'rational, tranquil and cheerful' from the outset and showed no signs of his previous moodiness and depression. He did not spend long in detention and, on his release in 1906 he became a solicitor's clerk, working for his father, who undertook to provide him with a home, a suitable education and employment. After William Rodgers died in 1910, Frank went into business with his father's business partner and his older brother William junior, who signed an undertaking to be fully responsible for Frank, to exercise constant care and supervision over him and to report to the Secretary of State any future symptoms that might indicate that he was a danger either to himself or others. Frank is believed to have married in 1909 and went on to have two children. He enlisted in the Royal Garrison Artillery during the First World War and is thought to have died in 1965. Queenie, the little sister he sought to protect, lived until her mid-nineties.

'Stop it our George'.

Northampton, 1904

After his wife Louisa died in January 1900, unemployed machine sewer George Scott Burrows was left to raise their six children alone. At about twenty-past eight on 17 February 1904, Burrows had to go out for a little while. At that time, five of the children were at home in Ivy Road, Northampton. His eighteen-year-old daughter Beatrice Mary and fifteen-year-old son George were reading newspapers in the downstairs sitting room, although Beatrice went out shortly after their father left, while eleven-year-old Elsie Jane, ten-year-old Thomas Gordon and eight-year-old Harry were upstairs in bed.

When Burrows returned home twenty minutes later, he was surprised to find the front door locked. Having used his key to get in, the first thing he heard was Thomas desperately calling out 'Daddy'. Taking a lamp, Burrows went upstairs, finding his two youngest sons hiding behind the locked door of their bedroom. 'George has been in Elsie's room' Thomas told his father.

Burrows went to check on Elsie and was horrified to see her lying on her side, her bedclothes saturated with blood. Burrows spoke to his daughter and gently wiped the blood from her face but the little girl was unresponsive.

Surgeon Henry Cropley was summoned and rushed to the house. He found Elsie in bed, her bedroom walls and ceiling plastered with blood and gore. Elsie's face was partly buried in her pillow and there were two large wounds on the right-hand side of her skull, one two inches long, just behind her right ear and the second one an inch long, just above the ear. The little girl's hands were cut and bruised as if she had tried to fight off an attacker. There were skull fractures beneath both wounds, and fragments of bone had been driven into her brain.

Elsie remained unconscious until her death forty-five minutes after the arrival of the doctor at her bedside. A subsequent search of the house by the police revealed no trace of her brother, George, but a blood stained axe was found in the cellar, with several human hairs sticking to the congealed blood on the head and handle.

Burrows was so disturbed by what he had seen that he fainted, thus it was some time before the police were called. When officers spoke to George's brothers and sisters, they were told that Elsie was a bright, cheerful and intelligent little girl, who was George's favourite – he was always buying her little presents from his wages from the factory where he worked as a shoe finisher. George was said to be of a morose and sullen disposition and was generally regarded as being 'mentally deficient.' He had twice run away from home, getting as far as London the first time, from where he was brought back by his father. On the second occasion, he tramped around Northamptonshire for a week. A quiet, shy and rather weedy young man, he was teased unmercifully at work about having to wear glasses, until he gave the main protagonist a good thrashing, after which he was left well alone.

His younger siblings were said to have lived in fear of him for some time and to have frequently complained about his conduct towards them. Nevertheless, when Elsie went to bed on the night of 17 February, she and George seemed on their normal friendly terms and kissed each other goodnight. Beatrice told the police that when she and her brother sat together in the front room, his behaviour had seemed perfectly normal. She had asked him if he wanted to go out and, when he said no, she decided to go out herself. Before leaving the house, she checked on her three youngest siblings and Elsie was then sleeping peacefully in her bed.

Thomas told the police that he had not fallen asleep and was aware of both his father and his sister leaving the house. Shortly afterwards, he heard his brother going to the cellar then walking upstairs, at which he scrambled out of bed and quickly locked his bedroom door. Asked why he had done this, Thomas explained that earlier in the evening, George had reprimanded him and Harry for making too much noise and disturbing his reading. He therefore thought George was coming to hit them, adding that he quite often did.

Thomas heard George go into Elsie's bedroom and hit her, telling police that the screaming girl repeatedly shouted 'Stop it our George'. When Elsie finally went quiet, Thomas heard George run downstairs and straight out through the front door. Too afraid to get up and go to Elsie, Thomas cowered in his bedroom until he heard his father return.

Gold Street, Kettering, (author's collection)

All Northamptonshire police officers were asked to be on the lookout for George and, on the afternoon of 18 February, PC William Thomas Dunkley was on point duty on Gold Street in Kettering when he saw a boy matching George's description. The boy looked tired, footsore and somewhat dazed but when Dunkley challenged him he readily admitted to being George Burrows of Ivy Road, Northampton.

'You had better come along with me' Dunkley told him, adding 'You know what for don't you?'

'Yes' replied George, allowing himself to be escorted to Kettering Police Station, where he was cautioned and charge with murdering his sister.

'I did do it' he admitted.

An appearance before magistrates resulted in George being committed to stand trial at the next Northamptonshire Assizes, as did the inquest held by coroner Mr C. C. Becke, at which the jury returned a verdict of wilful murder against him.

The proceedings opened at the Shire Hall, Northampton on 21 June 1904, the first time that newly appointed judge Mr Justice Bray had presided over the Assizes. Mr H. W. Disney and Mr Bernard Grain prosecuted the case, while, at Bray's request, Mr Bernard Campion defended. When the charge that he had wilfully murdered his sister was read out in court, George pleaded guilty. Campion immediately advised his client to plead not guilty but George made no response to the request from his counsel and eventually, Mr Justice Bray himself entered a plea of not guilty on his behalf.

It took the prosecution only an hour to present their case, after which it was left to Campion to speak for George. He informed the jury that the boy's only possible defence was one of insanity and called Mr Lee Fyson-Cogan, the medical officer at the prison where George had been detained pending his trial.

Cogan explained that he had been observing George ever since 19 February and had conducted several interviews with him. Cogan was of the opinion that George was '…a lad of defective mental organisation', who was affected by impulsive insanity and homicidal mania. It had been mentioned in court that George was an avid reader, both of newspapers and of the more lurid crime novels, several of which his father had taken away from him as unsuitable. Cogan believed that the reading of such sensational literature might easily have affected George's mind. Asked if George were perfectly rational, Cogan found it difficult to answer, telling the court that the boy seemed perfectly sensible on all matters except those connected with the murder, which he tended to treat with great levity. To date, nobody had been able to ascertain any motive for the killing of Elsie Burrows.

'Suppose you had examined the boy without knowledge of the crime – would you have said he was insane?' asked the judge.

'I don't know whether I should be prepared to certify him absolutely to be a lunatic but I should look upon him with grave suspicion' responded Cogan.

He concluded his evidence by pointing out that there was no family history of insanity and that he was satisfied that George knew the difference between right and wrong.

Dr W. Harding, the medical superintendent of the local Asylum, had examined George while he was imprisoned and reached the conclusion that the boy was certifiably insane. Although the prosecution argued that Harding hadn't even met George until four months after the murder, Harding was adamant that, taken together, all of the boy's symptoms added up to a case of homicidal mania. George was described by his father as sulky and sullen. He did not mix easily and was '…a little duller of comprehension than most boys.' At school, George had been prone to what were described as 'violent and inexplicable outbursts of passion' and, with his propensity for reading lurid literature, the evidence led Harding to believe that he suffered from homicidal mania, which could strike at any time, no matter how rational he appeared to be in conversation.

Addressing the jury for the defence, Campion reminded them that two medical witnesses had expressed an opinion that here was a boy who 'wanted watching'. In impulsive insanity, the urge to kill came and went suddenly and, to an untrained eye, a person subject to such impulses might appear rational. Campion seized upon the absence of motive as being illustrative of George's insanity, which led him to kill the little sister of whom he was especially fond.

For the prosecution, Mr Disney argued that it was a highly dangerous practice to assume someone insane just because he committed an act of violence, for which no explanation could be given.

In his summary of the case, Mr Justice Bray pointed out to the jury that every man was assumed sane unless the contrary was proved. In other words, the onus was on the defence to prove George insane.

It took the jury just twenty-one minutes to decide that George Scott Burrows was not guilty on the grounds of insanity and Bray ordered him to be detained pending his Majesty's pleasure. In due course, George was sent to Broadmoor Criminal Lunatic Asylum, but was released in 1920 and taken under the wing of the Salvation Army. Unfortunately, George was unable to get a job on his release and eventually, to avoid bringing further shame on his family, he travelled to Southend in the hope of finding work as a bootmaker. When this proved unsuccessful, in 1922 he attempted suicide by cutting his throat in a public baths.

The resulting wound was not serious and George survived to appear at the Essex Quarter Sessions, where he pleaded guilty to attempted suicide. The medical officer at Brixton Prison stated that George was suffering from severe depression, having found it difficult to adjust to the stress and strains of the world outside Broadmoor. Enquiries were made of the Salvation Army but, on this occasion, they were unable to help so, in his own best interests, George was sentenced to twelve months' imprisonment. He is believed to have ended his days back in Northampton, dying aged eighty-one in 1969.

'Our Beaty's on fire'.

Portsmouth, Hampshire, 1914.

Mrs Kate Challis of Highbury Street, Portsmouth, was described by her neighbours as being 'weak-minded'. Her estranged husband Joseph was a hawker, said to be a man of filthy habits, who had deserted his wife and children in August 1912, after a warrant for his arrest was issued for neglecting his children.

Kate was forced to take whatever work she could in order to support her family and on 26 January 1914, she was offered a day's washing. Asking a neighbour to keep an eye on her children, Kate left ten-year-old George and seven-year-old Beatrice at home alone. Before leaving, she supplied them with food, a warm fire and enough fuel to replenish it during the day. Unfortunately, the fire was unguarded, since Kate could not afford to buy a fireguard.

At about ten o'clock that morning, neighbour Mrs Johnson heard fearful screams coming from the Challis family's room. She rushed to see what the matter was, finding Beatrice's clothes burning, with George capering gleefully around her, apparently enjoying the spectacle and shouting 'Our Beaty's on fire.' Mrs Johnson tried to put out the flames that were engulfing the screaming child but was unable to extinguish them. She called for assistance from another neighbour, Mr Elcock, and between them they managed to bring the conflagration under control.

Beatrice was rushed to the Royal Portsmouth Hospital, where house surgeon Edward Sowerby found that she had extensive burns on her arms, shoulders, face, ears and upper back. Still conscious, she told her mother 'George did it, Mammy. He pushed me on the fire because he wanted to eat all the gravy.' George made no attempt to deny his sister's accusations, telling people that he had chased his sister around the room with a knife, before pushing her onto the fire and holding her there. 'She squealed when I put her on the fire' he recalled, adding that he had eventually pulled her from the flames and tried to put out her burning clothes. 'I know I was a bad boy when I put her on the fire.'

Beatrice died from shock and 'septic absorption' on 30 January 1914 and an inquest was opened by coroner Sir Thomas Bramsdon J.P. There was some debate about whether or not Mrs Johnson had ever been asked to keep an eye on the children - Mrs Johnson claimed that there had been no such request, although she conceded that Kate may well have asked her mother to oversee them. Kate Challis had given birth to eleven children, five of whom were dead, five being inmates of reformatories or industrial schools.

The eleventh child was George and he was well known to the authorities, having spent time in imbecile wards at both Portsmouth and Brighton hospitals. In August 1913, he was referred to Dr H. W. Morley, the medical superintendent at Portsmouth Infirmary. At that time, it was suggested that George may be suffering from epilepsy but Morley found no sign that this was the case. Instead George was categorised as '...an imbecile of the most vindictive, spiteful and malicious kind.' It was Morley's contention that George was not fit to plead, although he was obviously aware of the gravity of his actions and the fact that he had done wrong. Morley told the coroner that, although it would be too dangerous for George to be at large, with proper training and supervision, there was a fair prospect for improvement in his condition.

The coroner told the inquest that, in the eyes of the law, George was seen as an adult, who was deemed capable of committing crimes. It was obvious that George should be kept under restraint but unfortunately the Children's Act made no provision for this. Thus, the coroner advised the jury to pass the case to the Assizes, for further consideration by a judge. The jury debated briefly before stating that, while they believed that Beatrice's death came as a result of her brother pushing her onto the fire, they believed that the act was done without malice and therefore returned a verdict of manslaughter against the boy. Newspapers bemoaned the inadequacies of the Mental Deficiency Act, claiming that had George been placed under restraint when his vicious tendencies were first observed, his sister would have been spared a terrible death.

When George appeared at the Hampshire Assizes in February 1914, he was described as looking no more than seven years old and was not tall enough to see over the dock rails. Given a chair to stand on, he surveyed the court from his lofty position, smiling benignly at the people in the body of the court. Once again, Mr Morley reiterated that he believed George was unfit to plead or instruct counsel and the trial jury agreed. Having stated that he found it unbelievable that George had ever been released from the imbecile wards, Mr Justice Ridley ruled that he should be detained in Winchester Prison until his Majesty's pleasure be known. Ridley promised to communicate with the Home Secretary on the matter and in due course, George was sent to Sandwell Hall Industrial School near West Bromwich. On 6 May 1918, he was transferred to The Stoke Park Colony for Mental Defectives near Bristol.

'I am always thinking it was only a dream instead of it being true.'

Millwall, 1914

After finishing work on the evening of 6 November 1914, Robert James Clements met up with his wife Margaret to do some shopping. Having bathed her son, seven-year-old Hubert Turner Herring, Margaret left the boy at their home in Alpha Road, Millwall, under the supervision of his fifteen-year-old stepbrother Sidney George Clements.

When Mrs and Mrs Clements returned home at around 9.30 p.m. they found Hubert lying face down on the hearthrug in the kitchen, a pool of blood spreading around him. Robert Clements picked his stepson up and saw that the boy had what appeared to be a stab wound in the right side of his chest. A large, bloody carving knife lay beside him on the floor, along with a piece of white linen, which seemed to have been used as a blindfold.

A doctor was called and, as they waited for his arrival, Mr and Mrs Clements tried desperately to staunch the bleeding. Although in considerable pain, Hubert was still conscious and told his parents that a nasty old man had hurt him and that Sidney had gone to fetch a doctor.

When Dr Rome Hall arrived, he immediately organised for the injured boy to be taken to the Poplar Hospital, where he was subsequently operated on. Sadly, Hubert died on 9 November and a post mortem examination conducted by House Surgeon Harry Bertram Walker showed that the cause of death was blood loss from a stab wound that had penetrated his diaphragm and liver and caused the collapse of his right lung.

The Poplar Hospital (author's collection)

There was no sign of Sidney, although on searching the house, it was discovered that two Post Office Savings books, belonging to Sidney's older brothers, had vanished. When he failed to show up for his job as an office boy at Ocean Oil Wharf the following day, the police began an immediate search for him, enquiring at lodging houses and checking to see whether he had gone to his grandmother's house in Burnham-on-Crouch. It was quickly established that a withdrawal of ten shillings had been fraudulently made from each of the missing savings books.

On the morning of Hubert's death, Mr and Mrs Clements received a letter from Sidney, who told them that he was in Southend-on-Sea where he was attempting to enlist in the Navy. 'I am very, very sorry for what I have done to Bert but I hope he is all right' wrote Sidney. 'While I was cleaning the knives and forks I seemed to have gone mad all of a sudden and did what I did do and now I can hardly realise what I done. I am always thinking it was only a dream instead of it being true. Albert's bank book will arrive on Tuesday Dad. I went to Southend Coast Guard Station to try and join the Navy but they told me to go to Leigh-on-Sea recruiting office and also told me that they will ask you for a Report of me. I hope you will not tell them what I done because I want to join the Navy and if they find out what I done I won't be able to get in the Navy but in the cells. I find it is the best thing for me to do to get in the Navy so I hope you will help me. You have always got on to me telling me that you would put [me] in the Navy so I ask you to give them your consent as soon as ever you can. I expect you will receive a letter from Leigh recruiting office asking for a Report of me. So please do not tell them what I have done. Sid.'

The police telephoned their colleagues at Southend and at 12.30 p.m. on 9 November, they received a telegram to say that Clements had been arrested and was in custody. P.C. Henry Campkin was sent to Southend to collect him and, on the return journey to Millwall by train, Clements made a full confession, telling the constable 'I was looking round for some money while Bert was drawing in a book. I was afraid he would tell father. Then I had a feeling come over me. I must have been mad. I then knocked him down, tied a cloth over his face and opened his shirt and stabbed him with the carving knife. It must have gone in a long way. He screamed and tried to get up. I told him to lie down and I would fetch a doctor. I then left the house taking the two savings books belonging to my brothers with me.' However, once Clements was formally charged with the wilful murder of his brother by Detective Inspector Albert Yeo, he made no further comment.

Clements was taken before magistrates at the Children's Division of the Old Street Police Court on 10 November, where he was remanded in custody to allow time for an inquest on Hubert's death to be held. When coroner Mr W. E. Baxter eventually concluded the inquest on 19 November, the jury returned a verdict of wilful murder against Clements, who was not present to hear the decision, having refused to attend. By that time, the police had established that there was no history of insanity in the Clements family. It was agreed that Sidney and Hubert had always got on very well together - even sharing a bed - and that they had never been known to have a serious quarrel.

William Nelson, who taught Clements for two years before he left school, described him as a quiet, shy, retiring boy, who often had a dreamy look about him but was nevertheless intelligent. Nelson assured police that Clements was well-mannered, neat, clean and appeared to have been well looked after at home. 'He never gave any trouble at all while I knew him' Nelson concluded. His views were in almost direct contrast with reports of Clements's demeanour at the police court, where he was described as 'a thin, untidy-looking boy, with rather a vacant expression, who does not in the least appear to realise the gravity of the charge against him.'

Clements was tried at the Old Bailey in January 1915, where he appeared before Mr Justice Rowlatt. Counsel for the prosecution, Mr Muir, attributed the murder of little Hubert to the fact that Sidney bore a grudge against his stepmother, for taking too great a proportion of his eight shilling weekly wage for his board and lodgings. Mrs Clements denied this, telling the court that a great change seemed to have come over Sidney when he turned fourteen.

Mr Justice Rowlatt (author's collection)

The court was told that, in the run up to his trial, Sidney had been closely observed by the senior medical advisor at Brixton Prison. Dr Dyer had found the boy to be particularly bright and intelligent, adding that he had seen no signs of insanity whatsoever. However, it emerged that, shortly before the killing of his stepbrother, Clements had spoken with a friend about a boy of seventeen who had recently been hanged for murder. Clements asked his friend what would happen to a boy of fourteen or fifteen years old who committed murder. He would not be hung, the friend assured him, but would most probably spend about fifteen years in a reform school.

'There was nothing mad about the prisoner, nor was he a bad boy', Muir concluded, adding that he regretted to say that Clements spent a good deal of his time in 'picture palaces.'

The jury found Clements guilty of wilful murder. Mr Justice Rowlatt described the killing of Hubert as a '…wicked, cruel and cowardly act', telling Clements that had he been just a little older, he would have been hanged. Rowlatt sentenced Clements to be detained during his Majesty's pleasure, warning him that if he ever did anything similar again after his eventual release from detention, he would surely hang. 'Take my advice' concluded Rowlatt. 'Profit by the instruction you will receive in the institution to which you will be sent and try and grow up a decent man.'

It has proved impossible to discover what happened to Clements after his sentence. However, records suggest that he eventually married and went on to have four children, dying at the age of eighty-three. Hopefully, he heeded the judge's advice and grew up a decent man.

'I didn't do it on purpose'.

Nottingham, 1918.

At around ten o'clock on the night of 12 June 1918, a woman went into the outside lavatory of an empty house in Vickers Street, Nottingham, where, to her horror, she stumbled over the body of a little girl, lying face down on the floor in a pool of blood. She immediately informed the police and Detective Superintendent Atherton and police surgeon Dr H. Owen Taylor rushed to the house. They arrived shortly before midnight, when darkness prevented a thorough examination of the crime scene. However the child's body was cold, leading them to conclude that she had been dead for some considerable time. There was a large wound in her neck and her spinal cord had been severed. A blood-spattered boulder lay close by and torches revealed a diminishing trail of bloody foot marks from the outhouse, through the garden, to the gate leading onto the road outside.

The police were already aware that a little girl who lived less than fifty yards from the house in Vickers Street had been reported missing the previous evening. On 11 June, eight-year-old Rosalind 'Rosie' Adkin came home from school to Sycamore Road for her lunch, which she ate with her thirteen-year-old brother, Frederick. When they got back from school again later that afternoon, their stepmother was out. According to Fred, he and his sister ate tea together then, at a quarter to six o'clock, Rosie told him that she was going to a mission meeting at the nearby Mechanics Hall. Fred followed his sister to the end of the road to 'make sure that she didn't dawdle', before returning home.

Rosalind Adkin (author's collection)

At around nine o'clock that evening, Fred was playing out in the street with some other children when his stepmother came back. Mrs Gertrude Mabel Adkin asked him where his sister was and Fred explained about the mission meeting.

Mrs Adkin was anxious and told Fred that she was going to look for the little girl. 'You are not going alone, mother. I am going with you' he told her. Fred and his stepmother spent the entire night together searching for Rosie, as did many of the family's neighbours.

However, they did not go to the empty house and Rosie's body remained undiscovered.

On the morning of 13 June, Dr Taylor conducted a post mortem examination on the child, who had now been positively identified as Rosie by her father, William. Taylor found that Rosie's skull was extensively fractured and there were significant wounds on her forehead and neck. It was Taylor's opinion that her injuries revealed that she had been subjected to extreme violence of a maniacal character. Rosie had suffered four separate, distinct blows to her head, possibly inflicted with the large stone found near her body, which weighed almost 17 lbs. Taylor believed that the skull fractures and consequent brain damage were the cause of Rosie's death and that the wound in the neck, was made after death with a 'sharpish' instrument, such as a pair of scissors.

In daylight, it became obvious that the supposed bloody foot marks leading from the body had a more innocent explanation and the police consequently discounted them, saying that they were not what they had first seemed. House to house enquiries brought forward a servant in a neighbouring house, who stated that she had seen two children entering the garden of the house in Vickers Street at around 6.00 p.m. on 11 June. The girl was wearing a round straw hat, the same shape as the one that Rosie was wearing when her body was found and, although she believed that the little girl's male companion was aged between twelve and fourteen, the maid did not get a close look at his face and so didn't believe she would be able to identify him if she saw him again.

With this new information, the police went back to speak to Fred again. At first, the boy denied all knowledge of his sister's death but eventually made a full confession to Detective Inspector Watson telling the policeman that he had gone with Rosie to the lavatory at the empty house, picking up a stone outside. 'Rosie knelt down and the stone slipped out of my hands and fell on her, stunning her. I didn't do it on purpose. I then cut her at the back of the neck with a piece of glass, which I found under a bush in the garden and cut her neck with some scissors.' Fred told the police that he smashed the piece of glass on a brick and put the scissors in his jacket pocket, where they were later found. After killing his sister, Fred went home and put the kettle on to make tea. He played the piano in the parlour for a while, before doing the washing up, after which he went out to play.

At an inquest held by coroner Mr C.L. Rothera, the jury found a verdict of wilful murder by Frederick Bestall Adkin and he was committed on the coroner's warrant to stand trial at the Assizes. The boy made several appearances before magistrates at the Nottingham Guildhall and according to reports in the contemporary newspapers he had little appreciation of the seriousness of his position, even sleeping through some of his hearings.

It was no secret that Fred was an epileptic, who had a fit about every three weeks. According to his stepmother, his fitting made him both irritable and mischievous. Fred claimed to have suffered two fits at school on the morning of his sister's murder. After his fits, he was often unable to remember what had happened. He was a bright and affectionate boy but showed no shame or remorse for any wrongdoings. He frequently lied and stole from shops or from other people and punishing him did not have the slightest effect on his behaviour. Fred's older sister, Lily, was similarly afflicted with epilepsy, which was so severe that she was confined in a home for epileptics near Chesterfield. Fred himself had been assessed a year earlier, when it was decided that his condition was not quite severe enough to warrant his admission to an institution. Nevertheless, according to Dr Taylor, epileptics were liable to homicidal mania and often had no recollection of what they had done.

By the time Fred appeared at the Nottingham Assizes before Mr Justice Atkin, it was widely accepted that, although the boy was aware that he had done wrong in killing his little sister, his epilepsy may have prevented him from controlling himself. Even at the trial, it was obvious that Fred still had very little appreciation of his actions. In Fred's defence, his counsel Mr Norman Birkett suggested that a proper, merciful and satisfactory outcome to the trial would be for the jury to find that Fred committed the offence but was insane at the time.

In his summary, Mr Justice Atkin rued the fact that '...the boy was not put under proper restraint long ago.' The jury followed the recommendations of the defence counsel and found Frederick Bestall Adkin guilty but insane, at which the judge ordered him to be detained during his Majesty's pleasure, in order to receive treatment for his epilepsy, adding that if Fred were cured, he would ultimately be freed. It has proved impossible to trace what happened to Fred after his trial but he is believed to have died a free man in 1974.

'I want to give myself up'.

Gunthorpe, Near Peterborough, 1919.

Frederick Brown ran a dairy farm at Gunthorpe near Peterborough and employed his brother-in-law George Herbert Watkins as his dairy manager. Every day, Watkins shared the job of milking the cows with head cowman John Jacklin and fifteen-year-old dairy man, James Botten, who began working for Brown on 5 November 1917. James Botten did not like George Watkins, who was married with one child, and whenever Watkins was away from work, Botten told everyone that he wished he wouldn't come back again. Matters between them came to a head on 30 January 1919.

On that day, Jacklin arrived at 5.00 a.m. to milk the cows. Botten arrived and hung up a lamp, before leaving the milking parlour again. Jacklin began milking but when neither Watkins nor Botten came to assist him as they normally would, he left the cows to look for them. As he opened the sliding doors leading out of the milking parlour, Watkins fell through them, dead from a gunshot wound to the back of his neck. A later post-mortem examination carried out by Dr Egerton-Gray showed that he had been shot at close range, since the shot was clustered in a small group and had not begun to spread out.

Meanwhile Botten had walked to the police station at Thorpe Road, Peterborough, where he told Superintendent Slaughter 'I want to give myself up. I have shot a man named Watkins.' Asked if he had shot Watkins deliberately or by accident, Botten willingly admitted that he had shot Watkins on purpose, as he walked through the cow shed with a milk churn balanced on his shoulder. 'He was always wanting me to do so much work and threatening to knock me down if I didn't do so much' Botten explained.

In view of Botten's confession, it was a formality for both the inquest jury and the magistrates to send him for trial at the next

Northamptonshire Assizes, where he faced Mr Justice Sir Montague Shearman, with Mr L. W. J. Costello prosecuting and Mr J. N. Emery acting for the defence. Described as a tall, gaunt-looking youth, Botten crossed the court in a slow, shuffling gait and looked around vacantly, taking very little interest in the proceedings beyond pleading guilty to the charge against him.

The court was told that Botten nursed a long term grievance against his foreman Watkins, believing that he was expected to do too much work and that Watkins was bullying him. Botten was described by his employer and by head cowman Jacklin as being 'somewhat strange in his manner'. Both admitted that they had heard Watkins ribbing or 'jawing' Botten at times but denied there was any malice intended.

John Jacklin described the events of the morning of 30 January, explaining that the milking machine had a very noisy engine, which had completely drowned out the sound of the shot that felled Watkins. Describing Botten as a '…sulky, surly lad', Jacklin pointed out that this was the only time that the youth had ever hung up a lamp in the milking parlour.

Dr Egerton-Gray gave medical evidence about Watkins's injuries and, in cross examination, also gave his opinion that the development of Botten's head suggested that he was intellectually weak.

Botten's mother was called as a witness and, asked to take the Bible in her hand so that she might be sworn. 'I would rather not' she demurred. The judge told her that she was required to take the oath by law.

'The law took my children away from me' responded Mrs Botten. 'In God's name, I cannot oath my children from me.'

'Will you please take the oath' asked the judge testily.

'I cannot do it' replied Mrs Botten.

'Take the oath and do not be foolish. I am anxious to do what I can for you' insisted the judge.

'I am willing to do my duty for my children' conceded Mrs Botten, eventually taking the oath.

She told the court that she had been trying to separate from her husband and that magistrates had offered her a place in the Work House with her children but she did not want to go. Very few people had anything good to say about James Botten - a neighbour described his whole family as 'neurotic' , a Peterborough probation officer, Mr Campling, classed him as 'very reserved' and even the local vicar could find nothing to say other than that Botten was '…rather curious at times.'

Having heard all of the evidence Mr Justice Shearman told the court that a boy of fifteen-and-a-half was assumed by law to '…know what he was about' and was also assumed to be a person who understood the concepts of right and wrong, until it was proved that he was insane. Dealing with the question of insanity, Shearman told the jury that there was undoubtedly plenty of evidence of abnormality. However, that said, the judge imagined that every single criminal who had ever been brought before him showed some signs of abnormality and, in Botten's case, there was nothing to suggest that, in shooting Watkins, he did not know that he was doing wrong.

Thus, in the eyes of the law, Botten was assumed to be sane. The judge reassured the jury that, in 1908, the law had been amended so that sentence of death could not be recorded against a person who was under the age of sixteen. Therefore, if Botten was found guilty, he would be sentenced to be detained during his Majesty's pleasure and placed in the '…wide, just and merciful hands' of the Home Office to decide exactly what should be done with him.

The jury deliberated for five minutes in the jury box, before retiring, returning ten minutes later with a guilty verdict.

Botten was first sent to Wormwood Scrubs Prison for observation, then to Borstal, where he served three years. The Home Office was then approached to either release him on licence or send him to Dartmoor Prison and he is believed to have gone to join other young offenders at Dartmoor.

'What can they do to me for this?'

Llantilio Crossenny, Wales, 1920

On 11 June 1920, fifteen-year-old Primrose Catherine Alice Whistance ran into a police station and begged the sergeant 'Please come down at once. My Auntie…' When the sergeant asked her what the matter was, Primrose told him that her aunt had '…gone out of her mind' At the girl's insistence, police hurried to the isolated cottage at Llantilio Crossenny, ten miles from Monmouth in Wales, where Primrose had been living with her aunt, Sarah Ann White, for the past four years. According to Primrose, she and her aunt had eaten supper and gone to bed as normal on the previous evening. However, to the girl's surprise, Mrs White had unexpectedly roused her niece at three o'clock in the morning and told her to get on her bicycle and take a box of valuables to her mother, who lived about a mile away. Primrose left as soon as it was light at around five o'clock that morning and, when she returned to the cottage two hours later, she called out 'Auntie' but got no reply. Claiming to be too frightened to enter the house, Primrose immediately went for the police.

The downstairs of the cottage was seemingly undisturbed but when the police went upstairs, they found the walls of the bedroom heavily spattered with blood and brain matter. The fifty-three-year-old widow lay concealed beneath a bedspread on the floor, dressed in her night clothes. Her head was very battered and a stake beetle – a heavy wooden mallet - lay on the nearby windowsill, clotted with blood and hair. The police naturally made interviewing Primrose their top priority and now she added more details to her first account, saying that her aunt had been very restless and unable to sleep, tossing and turning constantly in the bed she shared with her niece. Telling Primrose – who she always referred to as 'Kitty' - to take the box of valuables to her mother, she instructed the girl to leave the front door open on her way out as she was expecting a visitor. She also told her niece that, if anything had happened in her absence, she must immediately fetch the police sergeant.

It was initially supposed that the motive for the murder was robbery. Mrs White had been widowed many years earlier and her husband Robert had left her sufficient money and property to allow her to live comfortably for the rest of her life, although his will stipulated that she should never marry again. However, when police searched the cottage, they were quickly able to rule out robbery, since several sums of money remained clearly visible. Meanwhile, Primrose seemed to be enjoying the notoriety, giving interviews to members of the press.

'I lived quite happily with my aunt' she insisted, 'and nothing unusual happened until Thursday [the day before the murder]. Then my aunt gave me a gold ring, which I had often wanted. "This is a keepsake' she told me, for you when I am gone. You make your home with your mother or with your aunt Bessie. I wondered why she spoke to me like that unless something was going to happen.'

The local police were quick to call for the assistance of Scotland Yard and Chief Inspector Holden and Detective-Sergeant Alfred Soden arrived in Wales on the morning after the murder to take charge of the enquiry. A post-mortem examination carried out by Dr Thomas Edward Lloyd confirmed the cause of Mrs White's death as fracture of the skull and laceration of the brain, caused by four blows, most probably with the beetle, which weighed almost three and a half pounds. In Lloyd's opinion, the first blow had been struck while the deceased was lying down, which had almost certainly caused her to fall out of bed onto the floor, taking her bedclothes with her. Because of the low ceilings in the cottage, Lloyd theorised that Mrs White's assailant had been a relatively short person. The weight of the mallet meant that it would not need to be wielded with a great deal of muscular strength to be an effective weapon.

Monmouthshire coroner Mr Herbert Williams opened an inquest but, after taking evidence of identification, he informed the jury that he had been specifically asked not to proceed with it and immediately adjourned the proceedings for a week.

Primrose was interviewed again and assured the police that her aunt always treated her very kindly and that they were on the most affectionate terms. Primrose stated that, after leaving school twelve months earlier, she now worked for her uncle James at Little Trighin Farm, although she returned to her aunt's house to sleep every night. Primrose's mother corroborated her daughter's story, adding that Mrs White treated her niece more like a mother would than anything else. Only the previous week, she had bought the girl a new bike and, several weeks earlier, had supposedly given her five pounds in bank notes and some silver coins. Primrose told the police that her aunt had very few visitors at home and received very little correspondence. However Mrs White had recently made some 'strange observations' almost as if she had a premonition that something bad was going to happen.

The day after the opening and adjournment of the inquest, the press reported that an arrest had been made, and the detention of a second person was pending. However the following day, the papers revealed that the arrestee was none other than Primrose, who appeared at the Police Court in Graig and was remanded in custody.

The main evidence against Primrose was her own confession. Initially arrested on 14 June by Soden, Holden and local officer Superintendent William Bullock, Primrose immediately denied any involvement in her aunt's death. Taken to the police station, she sobbed bitterly for twenty minutes before asking Bullock 'What can they do to me for this?'

'That's not for me to say' Bullock replied.

Primrose continued to cry for a further ten minutes then seemed to pull herself together. 'Now I am here I may as well tell you the truth about it', she told Bullock, who immediately began to write down her statement.

Primrose Whistance (author's collection)

'Well, I did murder my auntie', Primrose sobbed, explaining that about a month earlier, she had stayed out late, which upset the rather 'old-maidish' Mrs White. On 10 June, Mrs White seemed to have come to a decision to send her niece home to her mother and Primrose was afraid of losing her home. 'I woke up some time in the night and went downstairs into the kitchen and got the beetle. I went upstairs and hit my auntie with it. She fell out of bed and I hit her again.'

Primrose's mother now confirmed that, during the last few weeks, both Primrose and Mrs White had been to see her, each complaining about the other. According to Rose Hannah Whistance, her daughter claimed that her aunt had threatened to hit her, as well as saying that Mrs White was losing her mind.

When magistrates and the inquest jury alike returned a verdict of wilful murder against Primrose Whistance, she was committed for trial at the Monmouth Assizes, where she appeared before Mr Justice Lush. Brought to court from Cardiff Gaol, she was shielded from the public view by two wardresses, who swathed her head and neck in a grey shawl as she was led to the dock, where she pleaded not guilty.

The only real evidence against Primrose was her own confession and her defence counsel claimed that girls of fifteen or sixteen often had very little control over themselves and were unable to resist sudden impulses. 'Heaven forbid, however, that I should plead for a verdict of insanity against her because I cannot help feeling how greatly to her disadvantage such a verdict would be' he concluded.

Primrose's uncle referred to his niece as a bright, kindly disposed girl, adding that he had never seen her act at all aggressively. However, he conceded that she might well be physically capable of committing the act alleged against her and the jury eventually found her guilty, recommending mercy on the grounds of her youth and also the environment in which she had been brought up.

'If it were not that the evidence was clear, one would have wondered if it were possible for a girl of your years to have committed such an act upon one who treated you with kindness' said the judge, as he sentenced Primrose to be detained during the King's pleasure.

Described as 'a moral imbecile', Primrose was sent to Aylesbury Borstal Institution. By 1926, she had been released and was married. She is believed to have died in 1954, aged forty-nine.

Note: Some accounts state that Mrs White was found on her bed, rather than on her bedroom floor. Chief Inspector Holden is also named Helden in some reports of the murder while Primrose's mother is named as either Rose Hannah or Mary Hannah Whistance. Primrose is referred to as Katherine Alice Primrose Whistance and Primrose Katherine Alice Whistance. Official records appear to give a different spelling of her second name, citing her as Primrose Catherine Alice Whistance.

'Do come and face it.'

Abertillery, 1921

On the morning of 5 February 1921, Frederick Burnell asked his eight-year-old daughter to run an errand to Mortimer's seed merchants, to purchase some ingredients for the poultry food that he was boiling up. Since the shop was less than four hundred yards from the family home in in Earl Street, Abertillery, Burnell became worried when Freda hadn't returned thirty minutes later, particularly since he had promised her a penny if she was quick.

Burrell left his stove to go and look for his daughter. When he was unable to find her, the police were informed of her disappearance and, as news of a missing child spread throughout the town, people borrowed lamps from the area's collieries and began searching. Cinemas were contacted and a missing persons' appeal was broadcast at every film screening that evening. Newspapers published a detailed description of Freda and her clothing, stating that she was small for her age and had blue eyes, a fresh complexion and light brown hair, which was tied up in rags in order to curl it. When she left home, she was wearing a red serge cap with blue velvet trim, a brown coat, a blue 'turnover' with white stripes, a brown jumper, new combinations, black stockings and black button boots. She was also carrying a small chocolate brown leather handbag.

The publicity brought forth several potential witnesses. A woman claimed to have seen a little girl matching Freda's description walk past her house shortly after 9.00 a.m. At around the same time, the local baker shouted good morning to Freda, who smiled at him and continued walking towards the shop.

Doris Hathaway, who worked as a domestic for the Mortimer family, was upstairs when their shop bell rang at 9.15 a.m. She shouted downstairs to fifteen-year-old shop assistant Harold Jones, who went to attend to the customer. Freda was sold the poultry spice she asked for but was told by Harold that they had no pre-packed bags of poultry grit in stock, although he could sell it loose. Freda decided to run home and check with her father before committing to a purchase and left the shop.

On the morning of 7 February, colliery ostler Edward Thomas Lewis left home to go to work and, in a lane at the rear of Duke Street, he found Freda's body. The police were alerted and Freda was carried to her home, where doctors confirmed that she had been strangled with her scarf. She had also sustained a severe blow to the head and had been 'sexually outraged.' Fragments of chaff around the body and on Freda's clothes suggested that she may have been killed elsewhere and police initially focused on a nearby barn, believing that the little girl may have been lured there. This theory was supported by footprints in the soft mud outside the barn and an indent on a pile of chaff inside, as if someone had laid down on it, but the barn's owner subsequently pointed out that the building was precisely as he had left it the day before Freda's death. In addition, it was padlocked and the only key had not left his possession. Thus the police decided that Freda's body had probably been transported in a sack that had previously contained chaff.

An inquest was opened by Deputy Coroner Mr W. R. Dauncey and adjourned after identification of the body and testimony from Freda's father. A Salvation Army funeral was held on 10 February and, on the same day, police were informed that a handkerchief had been found in a storage shed belonging to shopkeeper Mr Mortimer, located only a short distance from where Freda's body was discovered. It bore traces of chalk dust and was peppered with distinctive small holes and, when it was shown to Freda's mother, she identified it as having belonged to her daughter Doris Ivy, who had a habit of chewing holes in her handkerchiefs. Mrs Susan Burnell confirmed that Freda had used the handkerchief to wipe chalk off a toy blackboard, minutes before leaving home for the final time.

The inquest resumed on 15 February and was further adjourned to allow the police more time to investigate. When it re-opened nine days later, the coroner was told that a policeman had walked the lane behind Duke Street in the early hours of 6 February. If Freda's body had been there at that time, he had walked straight past it without noticing it, although it was obviously dark and PC Wilfred Cox admitted that his attention had been focused on allotments at the side of the lane. On hearing of Freda's disappearance, miner Frederick Hedley Veal set about organising a search party. Veal had also walked through the lane at around 7.00 a.m. and told the coroner that he was absolutely positive that he would have seen the child's body had it been there.

Several people came forward claiming to have heard screaming at around 9.30 a.m. on the morning of Freda's disappearance. Fanny Manual, Edith Evans and Henry Arthur Duggan all heard a single scream, which was not repeated. Duggan actually believed that the scream came from inside Mortimer's shed and pressed his ear to a board covering a window. However, like Fanny and Edith, he heard no further noise and eventually carried on with what he was doing.

As one of the last people to see Freda alive, the police were naturally interested in Harold Jones and it was noticed at the inquest that his evidence frequently differed from the content of his original statement to the police. When pressed to explain these discrepancies, he claimed either to have been mistaken or to not know why his account had changed.

Several witnesses testified that Jones was at the shed on the morning of Freda's disappearance. It was his normal practice to visit the shed every day to feed the poultry kept there and more than one witness claimed to have seen him there at around 10.40 a.m. One such witness was ten-year-old Francis Gilbert Mortimer, the son of the proprietor of the shop where Jones worked as an assistant. Francis told the inquest that he often helped Harold to deliver orders. He recalled going to the shed with him at around 10.35 a.m. to collect a sack of potatoes and told the coroner that he waited outside for Harold.

After Francis's testimony, the coroner adjourned the inquest again, since it had already been sitting for more than seven hours that day. When it resumed, Francis was recalled as a witness and explained that it was not normal practice to leave the shop trolley outside the shed. Instead it would usually be taken inside for loading and, as far as Francis could remember, this was the first time that Harold had made him wait outside. Francis stated that, once the potatoes were loaded on the trolley, Harold sent him on ahead with them, promising to catch him up shortly. The boy also told the inquest that the door to the shed would not open as wide as it normally did, appearing to be impeded by a bulky sack just inside.

However, once Francis had finished giving evidence, his father was the next witness, immediately followed by his mother. Although Mr and Mrs Mortimer's testimony was seen as vague, unhelpful and evasive, both of Francis's parents gave evidence that contradicted that of their son, placing Harold Jones in the shop at the time of Freda's supposed murder. (Rhoda Mortimer actually told the coroner that her son's evidence was untruthful.)

The Mortimers were followed by William Ernest Greenway, who lodged with Harold Jones's parents at their home in Darran Road. On the night of Freda's disappearance, Greenway visited the theatre, arriving home at around 11.00 p.m. Greenway shared a bed with Harold and insisted that the boy could not possibly have got up during the night without him knowing. The police were of the opinion that Freda's body had been placed in the lane between 11.00 p.m. on 5 February and 7.15 a.m. the following morning and, according to Greenway, Harold was at home in bed during that entire period.

Edmund Clissett, Levi Meyrick and Alfred John Gravenor were next to give evidence. In turn, the three youths related going to the shed with Harold Jones at around 10.30 p.m. on the night of 5 February. They recalled Harold telling them that he had forgotten to lock the shed and did not want his employer to find out. After their evidence, the inquest was adjourned again and all three were recalled when it resumed the following morning, when it was suggested that they were all being somewhat economical with the truth.

After hearing medical evidence, the inquest was adjourned once more and when it resumed on 1 March, much of the day was spent questioning Harold Jones about inconsistencies in his statements. Proceedings were adjourned for a final time and on 7 March 1921 the coroner gave his final summing up for the jury. He pointed out that it was his belief that some witnesses had not told the truth when questioned, before asking the jury to decide whether they believed that Harold Jones had left the shop and gone to the shed between 9.25 and 9.40 a.m. on the day of Freda's disappearance. He reminded the jury that Mortimer's shed was strongly suspected to be the scene of the murder, since the handkerchief known to have been in Freda's possession had been found there. Only the Mortimers and their employees had access to this shed and only Harold's movements were unaccounted for at the crucial time.

After two hours, the jury notified the coroner that they were struggling to reach a verdict. Urged to continue debating the case, they finally agreed on a verdict three hours later; that Freda had been murdered by person or persons unknown.

In spite of the inquest verdict, Harold Jones was arrested later that evening and charged with the wilful murder of Freda Elsie Maud Burnell, telling the arresting officers 'I know it is all black against me but I never done it'. After an initial hearing before magistrates, Harold was remanded to Usk prison until his case was heard at Abertillery Police Court on 5 April.

In defence of Harold Jones, it was suggested that Freda might have been murdered by her father, angered at her having returned home without the poultry grit. Defence counsel William J. Everett also objected to a photograph of the interior of Mortimer's shop, claiming that it had been doctored. (The focus of his objections was that a piece of white paper had been placed behind the shed key in one of the photographs to highlight its normal position.) Although a note was made of the objection, the magistrates allowed the photograph to be admitted as evidence.

Throughout the two-day hearing, Harold Jones appeared calm and collected, until the moment when it was decided that he should be remanded in custody to face trial at the next Monmouth Assizes. 'I am not guilty' he insisted. 'I have always said I am not guilty and I am still saying it.'

The trial opened before Mr Justice Bray on 20 June 1921, with Jones confidently pleading not guilty at the commencement of the proceedings. Charles Francis Vachell K.C. and John Rolleston Lort-Williams K.C. undertook to prosecute the case, while St John Gore Micklethwait and Joseph Bridges Matthews K.C. acted for the defence.

Among the first witnesses to be heard were Harold Jones's parents, both of whom described their son as 'a good boy.' Both stated that Harold's bedroom door made a loud noise when opened and they were therefore certain that he could not have left home during the night of 5/6 February without their knowledge. Their opinion of their son was reinforced by Harold's headmaster, who told the court that he and the boy's teachers had always found him '…exemplary, respectful and of good moral character.'

Harold Jones (author's collection)

Since Harold Jones was only fifteen years old and much of the evidence against him was circumstantial, it came as little surprise when the jury took less than half an hour to find him not guilty. Released from custody, he was cheered as he left court and was taken to a nearby restaurant, where he made a speech from the balcony, assuring the crowds that he bore no grudge against the people of Abertillery for '…the horrendous ordeal I have been put through.' It is reported that a brass band played as he was then driven home in a charabanc, through streets lined with cheering, flag waving crowds.

Harold Jones's time as a local hero lasted precisely two weeks and was ended by an announcement from Superintendent Henry Lewis that the 'foully murdered ' body of a child had been found in the attic of Harold's family home.

Arthur George Little was supposedly one of the first to congratulate his near neighbour on his release from prison after the not guilty verdict. At 9.30 p.m., on 8 July 1921, Little was watching his eleven-year-old daughter Florence playing hopscotch in the street outside his house with Harold's sister, Flossie. He went indoors to attend to his son, Gwyn, who was ill in bed and, when Mrs Little went to call Florrie in for bed at just before 10.00 p.m., she was nowhere to be found.

An immediate search was begun for the little girl and Mrs Little called at the Jones household to see if Florence was there. The door was answered by Harold, who had obviously been disturbed while taking a bath. 'Florrie has left our house some time' Harold told the worried mother, before enquiring how Gwyn was.

As they had done for Freda, the entire village turned out to search through the night for Florrie but there was no trace of the missing girl. Although Harold Jones was among the searchers, not surprisingly, given that Florrie had been playing with Flossie Jones, the Little family were concerned about his possible involvement in their daughter's disappearance. Thus, after consultation with the police, Harold's father Phillip was asked to go to the Little's family home, where Superintendent Lewis informed him 'Somebody wants me to search your home.'

'By all means' Jones replied. Both he and Harold gave the appearance of fully co-operating with the police and the search was reaching its conclusion when PC Wilfred Cox happened to spot a smear on the upstairs ceiling. A closer inspection revealed that the walls of the landing appeared to have been recently washed or wiped.

Cox called for a chair and opened the hatch leading to the attic, immediately spotting the body of a little girl, who lay face down, with her head and shoulders wrapped in a grey shirt. It was Florrie, and when she was removed from the attic, it was apparent that her throat had been cut.

By that time, Harold had left the house and was playing outside in the street. When Florrie's body was found, Philip Jones went to fetch him. 'Come here sonny. They have found that body in our house.'

'I have never done it Dad' Harold insisted.

'You or me will have the blame. Do come and face it.'

Harold was charged with wilful murder, making no response to the charges. As he was taken to the police station, an angry mob of around five hundred people quickly congregated, ready to protest in the strongest terms about what they saw as the police's harassment of Harold, who had so recently been found innocent of murder. With the announcement by Superintendent Lewis that Florrie's body had been found, the crowd's mood changed dramatically and it was thought prudent to transfer Harold to a different police station for his own safety.

On 11 July, deputy coroner Dauncey was called back to Abertillery to preside over the inquest of Florence Irene Little. Two days later, she was buried at Brynithel Cemetery, her funeral said to be one of the largest ever seen in Welsh history. Almost 100,000 people are believed to have followed the coffin to its final resting place, although the mourners did not include the little girl's mother, who was too distressed to attend. Also absent was Florrie's paternal grandfather George Little, who was suffering from heart disease and died almost at the same moment as the funeral cortege left Darran Road.

On the day after the funeral, with their son in custody at Usk gaol, Mrs and Mrs Jones received a badly-spelled letter at their home, which bore a Manchester postmark and read: 'Dear Mr & Mrs

Jones, Just a few lines to say that I am very sorry to think your son has been blamed for what he has not done. It was me who killed the girl and I put the body in your house and am an Irish lad and had been working in Wales and are a Sinn Feiner and think it is very right to kill all I can of England lad and girls. I hope your son will be alright and get of. I feel sorry now I did it for a young lad to be blamed for me doing. If it had been the farther they blamed, I would not have cared for me and the farther had a few words at one time and I thought this was a good way to get my own back on Mr Jones. I am in Manchester but I am going out to Ireland to-night. My name is Duffy and if your boy Harold has to do time, he will be doing it for me. Thank god, so Mr & Mrs Jones you can rest your minds content. If your son is suffering it will be for the wrong I've done. God forgive me for allowing a lad of 15 to take my blame, Yours truly, Duffy. I am a man 46 years of age.' Although Philip Jones agonised over the letter, he was unable to recall any such contretemps with an Irishman in his past.

When the adjourned inquest resumed, Harold's nine-year-old sister Flossie flatly refused to attend. 'I begged and prayed of her this morning to come' Philip Jones explained to the coroner 'but she cried and cried and would not come and face them.' When Dauncey told Flossie's father that her presence was mandatory and threatened to send the police for her, Philip himself went home and fetched her. The sobbing child gave her evidence with great difficulty, recalling how her brother had sent her to the shop, first for cigarettes, then for a bottle of fizzy pop. When she eventually went into her house with Florrie, her brother was in the kitchen. Florrie left the house, after which Flossie went to visit her auntie and uncle and never saw her friend again.

As the inquest progressed, the evidence against Harold Jones seemed indisputable. According to county analyst Dr George Rudd Thompson, stains were still visible on Harold's blue trousers, even though obvious attempts had been made to clean the material. The stains, which were fresh, were comparable to Florrie Little's blood, as was congealed blood found on the blade of Harold's clasp knife. Witnesses placed Harold as being alone in the house at the critical time when Florrie died and, of course, her body was found in the attic of his home. It was almost a foregone conclusion for the inquest jury to return a verdict of wilful murder against Harold Jones, which was met by a heartrending scream from his mother. Harold himself seemed unmoved as he was led away to resume his incarceration.

An appearance before magistrates on 27 and 28 July followed the same lines as the inquest and led to Harold's committal to the Assizes for trial. However, on 27 October, just five days before the anticipated start of his trial, a statement was released to the press in which Harold confessed to murdering not only Florrie Little, but also Freda Burnell. As the Monmouthshire Assizes opened at the Shire Hall in Monmouth, Harold stood before Mr Justice Roche and pleaded guilty to the wilful and deliberate murder of Florrie. It was pointed out that, since Harold was only fifteen years old, the only sentence that the judge could pronounce was that he should be detained during His Majesty's pleasure. However, should the trial be delayed for any reason until after Harold's sixteenth birthday on 11 January 1922 then Harold could well face the death penalty.

Harold had made a detailed statement, which was then admitted into court as evidence. He described how he seized Florrie from behind as she was leaving his house and cut her throat, holding her head over the sink to catch the blood. Having wrapped her head in a shirt, he carried her body upstairs and placed it on a little table that he had dragged from his room and positioned beneath the loft hatch. Finding himself struggling to lift the body through the trap door, he fetched a rope from the back yard and hauled the body into the attic, before collecting a bowl of water and a cloth, which he used to remove bloodstains from the walls and the table. The only explanation Harold could give for his actions were that he had experienced 'a desire to kill.'

Maidstone Prison (author's collection)

Jones began his period of detention in Usk Prison, eventually being moved to Dartmoor Prison, where he remained until February 1923, when he was transferred to Maidstone Prison. He remained there until 1940, when he was sent to Camp Hill Prison on the Isle of White.

By November 1941, Harold Jones was in Wandsworth Prison, where he was being prepared for his release on 7 December 1941. Soon afterwards, Harold moved to London and adopted the name 'Harry Stevens'. He is known to have married and to have sired at least one child before his death in 1971.

Note: Witness Edmund Clissett is alternatively named Esmond in some publications. Records suggest that Edmund is correct.

'I didn't hardly know what I was doing.'

Redbourn, Hertfordshire, 1921.

North Common, Redbourn (author's collection)

Seventy-one-year-old widow Mrs Sarah Seabrook had lived in her cottage on the edge of North Common, Redbourn in Hertfordshire, for sixty years. The kindly old lady shared her home with her forty-six-year old son, Herbert, and two of her daughters, Olive and May, although all three went out to work, leaving Sarah alone at home. However, another daughter, Jessie Freeman, visited her every day usually between the hours of 9.30 a.m. and 4.30 p.m. May always came home from work to share lunch with Jessie and her mother, after which Sarah would invariably have an afternoon nap in her bedroom.

On leaving her mother's cottage after their midday meal on 27 January 1921, Jessie was particularly careful to ensure that the front and back doors were locked, since small sums of money had been missed from the cottage in recent weeks. Jessie went into Harpenden on her bicycle to do some shopping, returning at about 3.30 p.m., when she discovered that the key to her mother's front door wasn't concealed in its usual place. Worryingly, when Jessie looked through the front room window, the house appeared to be full of smoke, which was seeping out from the edges of the window frame.

Jessie managed to open the door using the key to her own house and found that a chair had fallen onto the kitchen fire and a sheet that had been resting on the back was burned to ashes. Jessie swiftly threw the smouldering chair outside, before returning to the house to search for her mother, who lay slumped on the floor close to the kitchen sink, her right arm in a bucket of water. Bleeding heavily from her head, Sarah was still conscious, although all she could manage to say was 'Jessie, Jessie', the words accompanied by thick bubbles of blood from her mouth.

Sarah was rushed to hospital at Hemel Hempstead but died that evening from her injuries. At the hospital, Dr Georgina Elizabeth Millar Davidson noted numerous wounds on her head, as well as a lacerated ear. Although Sarah had, in the past, suffered from two seizures, the doctor was of the opinion that the majority of her wounds were far too severe to have been caused by her falling or thrashing around in the throes of a fit. District Nurse Angela Moore, the first medically trained person to see Sarah, was under the impression that the elderly lady had suffered a stroke. Yet, given the amount of blood in the bedroom, Nurse Moore had grave doubts that a person losing such a great quantity of blood upstairs would be physically capable of getting downstairs, particularly someone as infirm as Sarah. The nurse accompanied the badly injured woman to hospital and was later to tell the inquest that during the journey Sarah held her hands up, as if trying to push someone away and begged 'Don't let him touch me' and 'Let me get up.'

The police were hampered in their investigations by the fact that, thinking that Sarah had simply suffered another seizure, her neighbours had scrubbed the kitchen clean. The investigating officers deduced that a violent struggle had taken place in Sarah's bedroom, in the course of which the curtain was torn and splashed with blood. There was a large pool of blood on the floor next to the bed and more downstairs, along with blood stains on some coats hanging in the kitchen at about the level of Sarah's head. A bent poker was found near to where Sarah had fallen, although since it had been given a thorough clean and burnish, it was unlikely to provide too much useful information. However, since the cottage ceilings were only 7'9" high, from the position of Mrs Seabrook's injuries, the police deduced that the poker must have been wielded by someone who was short in stature, since there were no marks on the ceiling. Jessie Freeman was adamant that she had used the poker for the fire on the day of her mother's murder, when it had been perfectly straight.

Officers from Scotland Yard were invited to assist the local police in their enquiries and started by speaking to the dead woman's neighbours. It was established that nobody had seen any strangers near to Sarah's cottage, in spite of the fact that the police had found a trace of blood on the back door, as well as footprints outside, as though someone had stood on tiptoe to peer in through a back window. Meanwhile, Home Office pathologist Bernard Spilsbury and Dr W.E. Gilroy conducted a post mortem examination, which revealed that Sarah's skull had suffered eight fractures and she had a total of twenty-eight scalp wounds, of various degrees of seriousness. Their position seemed to indicate that someone had repeatedly rained blows on her head while she was unconscious and thus unable to move. Spilsbury remarked that Sarah had an unusually thick skull and, if this had not been the case, he was sure that her head would have been 'smashed to a pulp.' As well as the injuries to her head, Sarah had a broken arm and broken bones in her hand, along with severe bruising on the right hand side of her neck.

The police were particularly interested in hearing from the occupants of the cottages neighbouring that of the victim. Such was the violence of the attack on Sarah Seabrook that it seemed inconceivable that her neighbours hadn't heard anything. Thirteen-year-old Donald Litton, who had fallen over and badly cut his knee the previous day, was in too much pain to go to school and was therefore at home alone next door all afternoon. He claimed to have heard no unusual sounds but told the police that he had spent almost fifteen minutes down a well in his garden, having accidentally slipped and fallen in head first. The well was twenty-seven feet deep, with ten feet of water at the bottom and the boy knew that calling for help was pointless, since there was nobody but him at home. He explained that he managed to brace his feet and back against the walls of the well and gradually inch himself up, adding that his coat and trousers were wet through when he finally managed to escape. Putting his wet clothes in the bath to drain, he was sitting by the fire in his underpants and nightshirt when his widowed mother returned home at 5.00 p.m.

Litton's story sounded highly improbable to the police, who admitted to being baffled by the case. Until the post-mortem examination indicated foul play, officers had first thought that Sarah Seabrook died either from a fall downstairs, a stroke or a seizure. Sarah got along well with everyone, apart from two elderly spinsters who lived nearby, although their advanced age and frailty made it inconceivable that they might have harmed her. It was difficult to find any possible motive for her murder, since she was very well liked in the neighbourhood and other than her meagre old age pension she had nothing of any value that was worth stealing.

On 2 February, Scotland Yard officer Detective Inspector Alfred Crutchett decided to interview Donald again and sent two local police officers to collect him. On the way to the police station, Litton began talking and, on their arrival, Sergeant Askew informed Crutchett that Donald now wished to change the statement he had made a few days earlier.

Donald Litton (author's collection)

'I want to get it off my mind. It has been worrying me' Donald told Crutchett, who immediately cautioned him, before asking him what he meant. Donald agreed to give a written statement and Crutchett asked him to begin by writing down that he had been cautioned, so that there would be no doubt in anyone's mind.

'I wish to clear my mind' Donald wrote. 'On 27 January, I walked up the garden of our house just after two o'clock. My mother had gone out. I wanted some money to go to the zoo at Easter. I went to the barn and got a hammer and put it in my pocket. I went to Mrs Seabrook's back door and found it locked. I pushed up the window and leaned in and pushed the bolts back. Then I pulled the window down and looked in the kitchen and front room. There was no one there and I found no money.' Donald continued by describing how he went upstairs and looked in the back bedroom. He opened the door of the front bedroom very slowly and saw Mrs Seabrook lying on the bed. As he was checking the bedside table for money, she suddenly woke up and saw him.

'I was very frightened and struck at her with the hammer…she was standing in front of the door and ran to the window and tried to open it. I caught her wrist and pulled her back on the floor. She knocked over a small table. I hit her with the hammer. Then I ran downstairs and up the garden and buried the hammer in Miss Weston's garden, behind the barn. I came back and went to the house again. She was coming downstairs. I pulled her over as she tried to get up again. I picked up a poker and struck her with it. She kept trying to get up and I struck her with the poker. The chair fell on the fire. I ran out and got down the well. I didn't hardly know what I was doing.

I thought I would try and drown myself. I got down by pressing my feet and back against the opposite sides of the well. When I got to the water, I let myself fall. As soon as I got into the water, I struggled and got my feet against one wall and my back against the opposite wall. I got up like this and went home. Nobody knew anything about it except me. I don't think I had any blood on my clothes.'

The police located the hammer, which belonged to Donald's mother, exactly where he said it would be and even though it had been buried, a few human hairs were still stuck to it. They also took plaster casts of the foot marks outside Sarah's cottage window, which were compared to Donald's hobnailed boots and found to match exactly.

Donald was charged with murder and although the inquest on Mrs Seabrook's death had opened and been adjourned, coroner Lovell Smeathman was taken ill and the resumption of proceedings was postponed. When it was finally concluded on 21 February, the inquest jury returned a verdict of wilful murder against Litton. Magistrates at the Children's Court in St Albans concurred, sending the boy for trial at the next Hertford Assizes.

As he stood before Mr Justice Rowlatt on 22 June 1921, Donald was described as a boy with '…intelligence beyond his years.' It was stated that the motive for Sarah Seabrook's murder was that Donald wanted some money to pay for a school trip to the zoo, which was going to cost seven shillings. Acting in Donald's defence, his counsel Mr Leighton insisted that so young a boy could not be held responsible for his actions but the jury disagreed and found him guilty. After sentencing him to be detained during His majesty's pleasure, Mr Justice Rowlatt informed the court that an offer had been made to adopt Litton but, as a judge, he had no power to allow it.

Note: The Detective Inspector from Scotland Yard is variously named as Crotchett, Crutchett, Crutchet or Crutchley. His signature on official reports indicates that Crutchett is the correct spelling. There is also some variation in describing the position of the Littons' home relative to Mrs Seabrook's cottage, with some contemporary newspapers saying that the two cottages were adjoining, others stating that the Littons' cottage was next door but one. Records suggest that the latter is actually the case.

'Quite young boys show murderous instincts.'

Henley-on-Thames, Oxfordshire, 1922

Sarah Ann Blake and her husband were joint licensees of The Crown and Anchor public house at Gallows Tree Common, near Henley-on-Thames, Oxfordshire. After Mr Blake's death in 1921, fifty-five-year-old Sarah decided to apply for the licence to be transferred to her name and by March 1922, the application had been approved and the transfer was imminent. The pub was situated in a secluded hamlet, with only thirty-five houses. It was the kind of place where everyone knew everyone else but Mrs Blake was a very private person, who tended to keep herself to herself. She had just one close friend – her next-door neighbour, Mrs Ellen Elizabeth Payne.

When Sarah was scheduled to go away to see to the licence transfer, Mrs Payne willingly agreed to run the pub in her absence. On 4 March, she went to see Mrs Blake for any last minute instructions and was surprised to find the front door of the pub still locked. No matter how hard she knocked on the door, or how loudly she shouted, Mrs Payne got no response from within and eventually, out of concern for her neighbour, she decided to force an entry into the pub.

Mrs Payne walked into an unbelievable scene of carnage. Her friend and neighbour lay dead in a pool of blood on the floor of the pub's kitchen, broken glass littered around her. Her hair hung loose around her face and every inch of her body was plastered with blood and gore, as were the kitchen walls. A blood stained butchers' knife lay on the dresser. A later post-mortem examination, carried out by Home Office pathologist Sir Bernard Spilsbury and Dr Luff from St Mary's Hospital, suggested that the deceased had put up a tremendous fight against her assailant(s). The pathologists detailed more than sixty wounds to Mrs Blake's head, hands, face and left arm. Her skull was fractured in four places and her right ear was almost completely torn from her head. One cheekbone was broken and, according to Spilsbury, one of her wounds looked as though someone had plunged a knife into her neck and 'worked it about.'

The first policeman to arrive in response to Ellen's call was PC James Buswell, who began a search of the premises. He noticed that there were two glasses on the bar, one containing mineral water and the other half full of beer. Yet although the pub appeared to have been ransacked, Buswell found substantial amounts of money in various rooms. A bowl and a biscuit tin in the kitchen contained almost £10 between them and more than £250 was found in the bedroom, along with a Treasury bond and a bank passbook with a balance of £465. Ellen Payne told Buswell that the bowl of money from the kitchen was normally kept in the pub cellar, where the policeman found more bloodstains, including some bloody fingerprints.

Police had soon questioned the occupants of every house in the small hamlet and initially came to the conclusion that the murderer or murderers most probably came from outside the area. Sarah Blake had last been seen alive at six o'clock on the evening of 3 March and it was estimated that she had been killed within two hours of that last sighting. Having eliminated all those living near to the pub as suspects and aware that anyone leaving the scene of the crime and heading towards nearby Reading would have had immediate rail access to almost anywhere in the country, Superintendent Wastie of the Oxfordshire Constabulary telephoned Scotland Yard and Detective Inspector Helden and Superintendent Ryan were sent to assist the local police.

Although the premises had been turned upside down, there was little evidence that much had been stolen. Nevertheless, the police were working on the theory that the motive for the murder had been robbery. The two half-empty glasses left on the bar seemed to suggest the presence of two men and, as the front door of the pub had been locked from the inside, and the killer(s) had left by the back door, it was thought that whoever killed Mrs Blake may have been familiar with the internal layout of the premises. The police appealed for a cyclist, seen entering the pub at a crucial time, to come forward. The man, who was said to have a pronounced stutter, was described as wearing a blue jersey and having a prominent Roman nose. Witnesses described his bicycle as having a high frame, with a punctured Dunlop tyre and a very bright acetylene lamp. On learning that Mrs Blake had been very afraid of a man that she and her late husband had met in America, the police requested assistance from their American counterparts.

The police had so far traced only two people who admitted to visiting the pub on the night of the murder. The first of these was a fifteen-year-old local boy named Jack Hewett, who had called in for a glass of 'raspberry champagne' and a bottle of ginger stout. When interviewed, Hewett told the police that he had been at the pub for only four minutes and that, while he was there, Ellen Payne's husband had come in for a beer, although he too had not stayed long.

Jack Hewett (author's collection)

Having conducted a search of the immediate area of the Crown and Anchor, within days of the murder the police had made some significant finds. These included the bloodstained key to the pub's front door, which seemingly materialised in plain view on a patch of grass in front of the building hours after the area had been carefully searched. The next find was an empty calico bag, identical to those in which Mrs Blake kept the pub takings. Then, on 14 March, the police found a rusted, open clasp knife in a hedge, about thirty yards from the pub. The knife bore what looked like bloodstains and there were several long hairs stuck to the blade, which were of a similar colour and texture to the victim's hair. When the knife was shown to Spilsbury, he agreed that it could easily have caused some of Mrs Blake's wounds.

Soon after finding the probable murder weapon, the police arrested a suspect. On 15 March, Robert Alfred Sheppard, a twenty-four-year-old woodcutter from Reading, was arrested and charged with having committed an unrelated burglary. At Reading Police Station, he asked to see Detective Sergeant Henderson, telling him that he wanted to talk about '…that Henley stunt on Friday night.'

Having been cautioned, Sheppard made a voluntary statement in which he said that he had been drinking in Henley on the day of the murder, with a man he knew as Jack Larking. Sheppard's companion told him that he knew of a place where they could get some money, offering to split the proceeds with him if Sheppard would act as his look out. The two men walked until they came to a pub and while Larking went in, Sheppard stood guard outside, ready to alert him if anyone came by. Sheppard told the police that, while waiting, he spoke to a passing cyclist asking him the time and was told that it was five minutes to ten. Describing Larking as being between thirty and thirty-five years old and having dark hair, Sheppard continued to say that Larking had been in prison several times. Although Sheppard stood outside the pub, Larking never returned and Sheppard eventually carried on to Reading and had not seen him since. Having subsequently read about the murder of Mrs Blake, Sheppard claimed to have worried a lot about it.

Knowing about the murder in the neighbouring county, Detective Sergeant Henderson sent a message to Superintendent Wastie, who arrived in Reading with Inspector Helden and Sergeant Ryan later that day, bringing with him the knife. Sheppard was visibly shaken when he saw it.

'Look here, what shall I get for the burglary?' he asked, adding 'I want to say something else. Give me a drop of water first.'

As Henderson rose to fetch him some water, Sheppard suddenly snatched up the statement he had just dictated from the desk. 'I did do the murder' he said, ripping his statement into little pieces and throwing them onto the floor. 'I had a bicycle which was a pinched one. It was earlier in the evening than I told you.' Sheppard went on to dictate a second statement, in which he admitted sole responsibility for the murder of Sarah Blake. When Helden examined the coat that Sheppard was wearing, he noticed what looked like bloodstains on the lining. 'I wiped them over since' Sheppard remarked.

Sheppard was taken before magistrates at Reading Police Court on 17 March, charged with burglary. The police offered no evidence and requested Sheppard's discharge, which was granted. On his release, Sheppard was promptly re- arrested by Inspector Helden and charged with the wilful murder of Mrs Blake.

An inquest on Mrs Blake's death had already been opened and adjourned. However, by the time coroner Mr Cooper resumed proceedings on 21 March Sheppard had changed his story and was insisting that the police had forced a confession from him. As Detective Sergeant Henderson told the inquest about Sheppard's request to see him, Sheppard angrily shouted to him 'Keep to the truth, Sergeant.'

Henderson went on to discuss Sheppard's second statement, after which Sheppard asked if he might question the policeman.

'Did I sign the second statement?'

'Yes' replied Henderson.

'Why did I sign it?'

'I read it over to you and asked if you wished to add anything to it.'

'Did you not say that if I signed the form, there would be no need for you to go and search my home?'

'No. I did not wish to search your home.'

'Have you spoken all the truth?'

'Certainly I have' Henderson assured him.

'That's enough for me that you are a lying hound' Sheppard accused him.

His outburst got him nowhere and he was summoned to appear before magistrates at Caversham on 7 April, charged on his own confession. However at that appearance, he was immediately released, although he was quickly arrested again on a charge of burglary at Reading. Once Sheppard had been discharged, Jack Hewett was officially charged with the wilful murder of Mrs Blake and took Sheppard's place at the magistrate's court. His story about being in the pub for only four minutes, during which time he purchased and consumed two drinks had never rung true with the police, who suspected that he had actually been in the pub for at least fifteen minutes and maybe more, particularly since, according to Hewett, Alfred James Payne had entered the pub, bought and downed his drink and left in that period.

The police had entertained suspicions about Hewett almost from day one. In the immediate aftermath of the murder, Hewett took to his bed with a mystery illness, variously reported to be mumps, pneumonia or flu. Nevertheless, the police called on him to take his fingerprints, for comparison to those found on glasses and on the pub's doorknob.

With Sheppard in custody, police had received information that Hewett had been seen peering intently into the hedge where the knife had been found. As he was known to have been in the pub on the night of the murder, he was interviewed again and shown the knife, although he denied ever having owned a similar one. Hewett, who lived within two hundred yards of the Crown and Anchor, worked as a labourer on a farm owned by Mr Paddick and, when Paddick's foreman Joseph Haines was routinely interviewed on 4 April, he stated that he believed the knife to be Hewett's. Haines was completely certain in his identification of the knife, having borrowed it from the boy during February.

Hearing this, the police went straight to Hewett's place of work finding him in a stable. They questioned him again about the ownership of the knife and, although Hewett continued to deny that it was his, he was to spend five hours with the police in the stable and, by the time the interview terminated, Superintendent Wastie had a signed confession.

Hewett told the police that he had been in the pub at six o'clock on the evening of the murder. Mr Payne had come in for a beer and left soon afterwards. Alone in the pub with the landlady, Hewett said he picked up an iron bar and struck her with it. There had been a fierce struggle, during which he had stabbed Mrs Blake with the knife, which he now admitted was his. He then washed his hands in a bucket of water in the cellar, locked the front door and went home, throwing the key down in the garden and disposing of the knife in the hedge. Hewett admitted 'I don't know what made me strike Mrs Blake but when I struck her I could not stop.' He admitted to stealing a few coppers from the house, adding that he had spent them on dried dates.

Hewett was committed for trial at the next Oxfordshire Assizes, appearing before Mr Justice Shearman on 22 June 1922, with Mr J. B. Matthews and Mr G. Milward prosecuting. He was defended by Mr Thomas Gates and Mr A. E. Godson, his defence paid for by a wealthy and philanthropic countess, who read about the case in the newspapers and contacted his parents offering financial assistance.

It had always been assumed that the motive for Mrs Blake's murder was robbery, although the police had never been able to find any evidence to support this theory. However, on 25 April, a Mrs Wheeler reluctantly made a statement, concerning a visit she had made to the pub in January of that year. As Mrs Wheeler was entering the pub, Jack Hewett was leaving and Mrs Blake called after him 'Now, Jack, remember the next time'. Once Hewett had gone, Mrs Blake explained that she had just caught him in her cellar '…at her money' and had warned him that if she ever caught him again, she would prosecute him. Mrs Wheeler asked if Hewett had taken any, to which Mrs Blake replied 'He did not have the chance to.'

In the course of the trial, Hewett took the stand and gave an account of his movements on the night of the murder. He told the court that a naturalist had given him a shilling for finding two squirrels' nests and he had decided to call in at the pub that evening to spend some of his money. There he bought a 'raspberry champagne' and a ginger stout, for which he paid 3d each.

Mrs Blake was alone at the pub when he arrived but Mr Payne had come in very shortly afterwards and drunk some beer. Hewett said that he left the pub at the same time as Mr Payne and gone to Smith's shop, which served as a meeting place for the young people of the village. On his way to Smith's, Hewett said that he had met his mother.

After hanging around aimlessly at Smith's in the rain for an hour and twenty minutes, Hewett told the court that he went home. When he got there, his mother sent him back to The Crown and Anchor to buy beer for his father but the pub was in darkness when he arrived and he had assumed that Mrs Blake had closed up and gone to bed, so continued on to another pub for his beer.

Hewett reverted to denying that the knife found in the hedge belonged to him, insisting that he didn't have a knife on him on the night of the murder, having lent his to his father the previous evening. Questioned further, Hewett told the court that he had sold the knife that he lent to Joseph Haines shortly before the murder, although he couldn't recall to whom he sold it, how much he got for it or even where the transaction had taken place. He admitted that marks resembling bloodstains had been found on his clothing but pointed out that he often killed chickens or rabbits.

Asked why on earth he had signed a confession, Hewett claimed that he had never even read it. He alleged that Wastie had written something down in his note book and told him that if he didn't sign it, he would be locked up. Hewett appeared to believe that if he signed his name to what was written in the note book then he would be allowed to go home.

Instead he was taken to Caversham Police Station and interrogated by PC Buswell, who asked him what he had done with the piece of iron. Hewett denied ever having had a piece of iron. He told the court that he had never been cautioned, nor had the police read the statement he was supposed to have made back to him. They had just handed him a pencil and told him to sign the note book page.

'I have never struck Mrs Blake' he insisted to the court.

Addressing the court for the prosecution, Mr Matthews asserted that if the story that Hewett was telling was true '…the police administration of the whole affair would be infamy too black for description.' Could the jury really believe that all four officers involved had committed such terrible perjury, he asked?

Matthews drew the jury's attention to the alleged sale of the knife, asking them if it were at all possible for Hewett to have sold the knife without recalling to whom he had sold it, how much he got for it or even where he was when the deal took place. According to Matthews, the sale of the knife was a cock and bull story, invented by Hewett to deny ownership of the murder weapon.

For the defence, Mr Gates told the jury 'Police officers do not wear a halo and do not always speak the truth' He asked them to consider why Hewett would have signed a confession if no inducement had been offered for him to do so.

'A confession should not be used against a person unless it was made properly, without any undue influence' continued Gates. To call this confession voluntary was a mockery, since the police played a cat and mouse game with the defendant and had not arrested him because, had they done so, they would not have been able to question him. Gates suggested that this was a case of Scotland Yard versus the local constabulary and that there was a great deal of jealousy and rivalry between the two parties, resulting in a desire to secure a conviction regardless of the facts.

Where was the cyclist, who had been seen by several witnesses to enter the pub at half-past seven? Why had he never come forward? Why were Hewett's fingerprints not found at the pub? And where was the iron bar, with which the defendant was alleged to have struck Mrs Blake and which had never been found?

In his summary of the evidence for the jury, Mr Justice Shearman pointed out that it was not unusual for so young a boy to commit such a crime. 'Quite young boys show murderous instincts' stated the judge, adding that, if convicted, Hewett was too young for the death penalty to apply. The crux of the defence case, explained Shearman, was that four police officers had committed perjury here in court and had fabricated a story in order to obtain a conviction. It was up to the jury to decide whether they believed such a thing could happen.

The jury deliberated during the luncheon interval, returning to pronounce Jack Hewett 'Guilty'. In view of his age, he was ordered by the judge to be detained during the King's pleasure. He was initially sent to Dartmoor Convict Prison but was then transferred to

Maidstone, where he became great friends with the Abertillery murderer Harold Jones.

Discharged on licence on 30 May 1932, with help from his solicitor, Hewett soon found employment as a garage assistant, remaining in that position until his employer went bankrupt. Married and living in Newbury, he was able to purchase a lorry, taking over several of his former employer's contracts. Reports to the Home Office state that he was able to make a good living for himself and his family.

Note: There are some minor discrepancies in contemporary accounts of the murder, with some newspapers stating that Ellen Payne initially broke into the pub and found Mrs Blake's body, while others report the first entrant to have been PC Buswell. The person drinking in the pub on the night of the murder is variously described as Ellen Payne's husband or brother-in-law. Helden, the officer from Scotland Yard is variously referred to as both Detective Inspector and Chief Inspector, his name given as Helden, Elden, Heldon and Holden. Jack Hewett's surname is also spelled Hewitt.

'I have been going to do it ever so many times.'

Waddingham, Lincolnshire, 1931.

Waddingham, Lincolnshire (author's collection)

James William Jacklin farmed Holme Farm in Waddingham, Lincolnshire, in partnership with his son, Robert James Jacklin. On 3 October 1931, as he did every morning, James called in at his son's isolated farmhouse expecting to begin the day's work. He immediately noticed that his son's bicycle was missing from the outhouse where it was normally kept. Unusually, the house was locked up and, since there was no response when he knocked on the door and shouted beneath the bedroom windows, Jacklin broke in.

Entering the kitchen, Jacklin found a quantity of smouldering straw that had apparently been spread around the floor and set on fire. A rug was also burning and, having stamped out the flames, Jacklin became aware of his eighteen-month-old grandson Maurice upstairs, crying pitifully for his 'Mamma'. Jacklin ran to see what the matter with him was and recoiled in horror at the ghastly scene that met him.

Maurice's mother, thirty-year-old Annie Priscilla Jacklin lay dead in bed, having been shot through the mouth at close range. On the floor lay her twenty-eight-year-old husband. Although half of his head had been blown away by a blast from a shotgun, Robert Jacklin was still breathing and tried desperately to raise himself on one elbow to speak to his father.

Mrs Jacklin with Maurice (author's collection)

Without even pausing to grab his grandson from the cot by his parents' bed, Jacklin ran to the village to summon help. One of the first people to arrive at Holme Farm was district nurse Miss Anne

Elizabeth Walters who, after carrying baby Maurice downstairs, did what she could to tend to his father until Dr William Anderson sent him to Lincoln County Hospital. Meanwhile, Superintendent Dolby arrived to take charge of the police investigation.

Lincoln County Hospital (author's collection)

William Jacklin immediately informed Dolby that there should have been another person on the premises. Sixteen-year-old Harold Smith was the son of Robert Jacklin's half-sister and had been living and working on his step uncle's farm since January 1931. There was no sign of him at the house, although his bed had obviously been slept in. The police were very anxious to talk to Smith and issued the following description to the local newspapers: 'About 5'7" or 5'8" in height, fair hair, slim build, protruding teeth, walks with a slovenly gait and may have his employer's bicycle in his possession. The machine has been renovated recently. It is thought he may have attempted to join the Army, as he has recently spoken to friends of enlisting.'

With the search for the missing Smith underway, the police began a detailed examination of the Jacklins' bedroom. A candle still burned in a candlestick placed close to the bed and there were two opened boxes of matches close by, one of which was filled with blood. On the floor lay two spent shotgun cartridges, one 'Glandford' brand, which was yellow in colour and one that was salmon pink. The bedroom window was open and a trail of blood led from the bed to the windowsill and had trickled down the outside of the house, as though someone bleeding heavily had opened the window and leaned out. The police deduced that, having been shot, Robert Jacklin had somehow got to the window and opened it to try and get help, before going back towards the bed. However, the farmhouse was so isolated that there was little possibility of anyone hearing him, even if he did manage to call out.

A search of the area around the farmhouse revealed a number of items hidden nearby in gorse bushes. These included some articles of clothing, among which was a brown coat. In the coat pockets were six pound notes, a ten shilling note, a cheque for £10 made payable to Mr Jacklin and Robert Jacklin's chequebook. The police suspected that Smith had shot his aunt and uncle and, having taken property and hidden it in a safe place for later collection, had attempted to set fire to the house to destroy evidence.

The appeal for information on Smith's whereabouts produced a flurry of information from the public. The police learned that at 7.30 a.m. on 3 October, he had called in at Mr Bradshaw's newsagent's shop and purchased a Hull newspaper. Bradshaw's shop was at Worlaby, roughly four miles from Holme Farm, and according to the newsagent, Smith was riding a bicycle. Smith's next sighting was at 9.00 a.m. by farmer Thomas William Farrow of Woodlands. Smith spoke to Farrow regarding a vacant position as a milkman, telling Farrow that he had been unemployed for the previous three months, before which he had worked as a horseman. He claimed to have previously worked as a milkman and offered to produce references. He seemed very anxious to get the job, so much so that he was reluctant to go back to Holme Farm in order to collect his clothes.

However, he did produce references purporting to be from a man named Smithson and, finding them satisfactory, Farrow gave him the job. (Although Smithson had once employed Smith, he had never written a reference for him.)

When this information filtered back to the police at Brigg, PC Smith (no relation) promptly commandeered a bus and set off for Wrawby. On the way, Smith passed his quarry riding a bicycle. The constable stopped the bus and arrested Smith, who told him 'I wish to say nothing about it now.'

Taken to Brigg Police Station, Harold Smith told the police that he did not wish his mother and father to be present, before voluntarily making a detailed statement. According to Smith, he went downstairs at around 4.30 a.m. on the morning of 3 October. Having searched in the cupboard for cartridges, he took the gun and walked upstairs to his uncle and aunt's bedroom.' I stood for four or five minutes outside the bedroom door where Jacklin and his wife and baby were sleeping' he continued. 'I then stood inside the doorway, wondering whether to do it or not. At last I touched the trigger and the gun went off. I shot Mr Jacklin first. The missis looked up and I shot her as well. I got an armful of straw and took it inside the house. I left a piece of candle with the straw on the hearthrug. We had been uncomfortable since last March. I was expecting more trouble as I had forgotten to put some straw in the hens' nest. That is why I shot them. I was expecting some more trouble. I ran away once before and they fetched me back. Robert Jacklin took some money off me. He said he did it for devilment. I have been going to do it ever so many times. I ought to have shot myself. I thought the house would be burned down and I should hear nothing more about it' he explained.

Smith was charged with the wilful murder of Annie Priscilla Jacklin and appeared at Brigg Police Court, where magistrates remanded him in custody for eight days to allow the police more time to investigate and to send details of the case to the Director of Public Prosecutions. Robert Jacklin died during the night of 5/6 October and Smith appeared before magistrates on 13 October charged with double murder. Not surprisingly, given his alleged confession, Smith was committed to appear at the Lincolnshire Assizes on 5 November 1931.

Mr Justice MacKinnon (author's collection)

His trial was presided over by Mr Justice MacKinnon, with Mr E. W. Cave K.C. and Mr E Ward prosecuting the case for the Crown. Mr H. H. Joy K.C. and Mr W. Carter acted as Smith's defence counsels. Smith was tried for Mrs Jacklin's murder only, the charge of wilfully murdering Robert Jacklin held in abeyance pending the outcome of his trial for the first count of murder.

Cave opened by describing the tragic events of 3 October and Smith's subsequent arrest. The court was told that during a post-mortem examination on Mrs Jacklin, shotgun pellets and cartridge pads were extracted from her brain that were identical to those belonging to her husband, which were normally kept in a cupboard downstairs. One of the spent cartridges found in the Jacklins' bedroom was a 'Glandford' brand and auctioneer Robert Montague Holmes recalled visiting Holme Farm on 22 September 1931. Holmes testified that he had an opened box of around twenty-four 'Glandford' cartridges in his unlocked car at the time. His evidence was corroborated by gunsmith Charles Alfred Leonard, who recalled selling the box to Holmes earlier that day, adding that it was the only box of that brand of cartridges that he had sold. Leonard identified the shot removed from Robert Jacklin as Glandford No 5 and confirmed that, at the request of the police, he had examined Jacklin's double-barrelled shotgun and found that it had recently been fired.

James William Jacklin was forced to relive his ordeal on the morning of the murders, describing how he found the carnage at his son's home and rushed for help. The court learned that Jacklin's shotgun, which had so recently been fired in the Jacklins' bedroom, was found propped up in the corner of a coal house. Having given his evidence, Jacklin was then questioned by defence counsel Mr Joy.

It emerged that Harold Smith was paid only 6d a week for his work on his uncle's farm.

'Was that all that your grandson was worth?' Joy asked

'We let him have what his father said he should have. Latterly I believe it was 6d a week' confirmed Jacklin.

Joy then asked some questions about Robert Jacklin's temperament. James Jacklin denied allegations that he and his son and daughter-in-law didn't get on. He also refuted Joy's claims that Robert was '...a surly sort of person', who was prone to bouts of depression and anxiety after a bad day at market.

District Nurse Annie Elizabeth Walters described carrying baby Maurice downstairs and tending to his father until the doctor arrived. She added that, two days later, she observed bruising on Maurice's face, on the side that would have been nearest to his parents' bed as he slept in his cot. Dr Anderson described being called to the farm and finding Robert Jacklin unconscious and suffering from severe gunshot wounds to his face. When Anderson attempted to rouse Jacklin, the injured man did not seem to appreciate that anything untoward had happened.

'It would have been quite possible for Jacklin to have shot himself and his wife?' Mr Joy asked.

'Leaving aside the other evidence – the murder weapon being found in an outhouse, the wounds on Jacklin's forearm, believed to have occurred when he raised his arm to try and protect his head and the fact that a fire was set downstairs – then yes, it would have been possible' conceded Anderson.

The court then heard an account of Harold Smith's movements in the aftermath of the shootings, including the revelation that, when apprehended, he was wearing a pair of Robert Jacklin's boots. Inspector Davies testified to searching the area around the farmhouse and finding the box of clothes, cheques and money concealed in a gorse bush. PC Smith and Superintendent Dolby then spoke about Smith's arrest and the subsequent statement he had given at Brigg Police Station, after which the prosecution rested and the defence called Harold Smith into the witness box.

In spite of the confession he had given when first arrested, Smith now claimed to have had nothing whatsoever to do with the shootings. He told the court that he had lived in Waddingham with his family and, after leaving school, worked on various farms in the neighbourhood, before going to work for Jacklin in January 1931.

Asked if he got on well there, Smith admitted that he didn't. In fact, he claimed to have been so unhappy that he ran away in the summer of 1931, but was taken back by his father.

Smith stated that, on the night of 2 October, he went to bed at about 8.30 p.m. and was woken by the sound of a gunshot, which he believed came from the Jacklins' bedroom. He dressed and walked down the landing to investigate and, by the light of the burning candle he could see Annie and Robert Jacklin lying in bed, both suffering from severe gunshot wounds. The gun was lying against the bed and Jacklin's hand was stretched out towards it.

'Did you use the gun that night or ever?' Mr Joy asked him.

'No, sir' replied Smith.

He continued to state that he had taken the gun out of Jacklin's reach and placed it downstairs where it belonged.

'What about that part of the statement to the police where you say you did the shooting? Is that true?'

'No, sir, it is not. I thought it would help me through it. I thought I should only get a light sentence as I was only a young lad.'

'So, you are saying that you had nothing to do with the shooting?'

'That's right, sir. But I did not think my word would be believed against so many.'

Joy then asked about setting the fire and again, Smith readily admitted that he had done it.

'Did you know there was a little child in the room?' asked Joy.

'Yes, but I did not know it was alive' Smith insisted.

Although the defence tried their hardest to convince the jury that Robert Jacklin had shot his wife and then himself, the evidence against Smith was compelling. Even so, he seemed unable to comprehend the gravity of his situation and chatted amicably to a prison warder as the judge addressed the jury. After a brief deliberation, the jury returned to pronounce Smith guilty, although with a strong recommendation to mercy on account of his youth. Nevertheless, Mr Justice MacKinnon was left with no alternative but to pronounce sentence of death on Harold Smith, who left the dock without showing any reaction and walked smartly back to his cell.

The death sentence awarded to Smith was to be the first issue tackled by newly appointed Home Secretary Sir Herbert Samuel (left). Although sixteen-year-olds were considered to be legally adults, it was not common practice in England and Wales to execute young offenders. It was at least forty years since a person under the age of sixteen had been executed and only five eighteen-year-olds had been executed since 1895. Given that Smith's guilty verdict had been tempered by a strong recommendation to mercy by the trial jury, it came as no surprise when Samuel announced the commutation of the death sentence to one of life imprisonment. Smith was released on licence on 16 June 1941.

Note: Some newspapers name James William Jacklin as Robert Jacklin senior. There is also some discrepancy regarding the

Jacklins' son Maurice, whose age is given as both eighteen months and thirty months. Since Robert and Annie Jacklin had only been married for three years at the time of their deaths, the younger age is most likely.

'I am a murderer.'

Newcastle-upon-Tyne, 1968.

By 1968, the old terraced houses in Newcastle-upon-Tyne were being demolished to make way for new homes. In the slum district of Scotswood, many condemned houses waited their turn to be razed to the ground and replaced by new high rise flats, among them 85 St Margaret's Road. On the afternoon of Saturday 25 May, three boys went into the boarded up house looking for timber to make a pigeon coop. However what they found in the rear upstairs bedroom was a dead child, who lay flat on his back, his arms above his head.

The three boys ran out of the house and spoke to two men who were working in the street. Only an hour ago, the men had given four-year-old Martin George Brown a biscuit – now, they tried desperately but unsuccessfully to revive him. As they struggled, Walter, one of the boys who had found the child's body, leaned against the window, trying to quell his nausea and to stop himself from fainting. He noticed two little girls walking purposefully towards the house and recognised them as thirteen-year-old Norma Joyce Bell and her ten-year-old next door neighbour, Mary Flora 'May' Bell. (The two girls were not related.)

As they approached the house, Mary asked 'Shall we go up?'

'Yes, let's' replied Norma.

The two girls scrambled through the window of the adjoining derelict house, walked through to the back yard then climbed over a dividing wall between the two properties. Walter intercepted them as they walked up the stairs, spreading his arms to prevent them from walking into the bedroom. However, the two girls peered past him to see the body, before they were told to leave in no uncertain terms.

Once back on the street, the girls walked to Martin Brown's auntie's house. 'One of your sister's bairns has just had an accident' Mary told her. 'We think it's Martin but we can't tell because there's blood all over him. Shall I show you where it is?'

Martin's mother, June, was fetched and Mary helpfully offered to show her how to get into the house where her son lay. As she ducked through the hole in the wall of the outbuildings into the yard, an ambulance man came out of number 85, carrying her son's body in his arms.

As many children did in the 1960's, four-year-old Martin had left home immediately after eating his breakfast to roam the streets. He spent some time chatting to workmen, before going to his auntie's house, where he was given eggs on toast by his grandmother. From there he went to see his father to ask for money for a lollipop. At around 3.15 p.m. he was queuing to buy sweets when his auntie saw him again. When Martin was reprimanded by the shopkeeper for having dirty hands, she took him back to her house for a wash and a treacle sandwich, before he was off on his travels again. By 3.30 p.m., he was dead.

A post-mortem examination yielded few clues. Some empty pill bottles had been found in the bedroom of the derelict house but Martin's stomach contents tested negative for drugs and poison. It was suggested that, since he had once fallen downstairs, he may have died from fright at finding himself at the top of the staircase. The only thing the pathologist found was a small brain haemorrhage, of the kind normally associated with strangulation. Yet there were no marks at all on the little boy's throat, neither did he have any wounds nor unusual bumps and bruises. The police concluded that Martin's death was accidental and, at the subsequent inquest, the jury returned an open verdict. This provoked an immediate reaction from the community, who took to the streets in droves to protest about the dangerous demolition sites and derelict buildings that proliferated in the area.

Just before Martin's funeral, Mary and Norma went to his house and asked to see him. Martin's mother reminded the girls that the boy was dead, at which Mary replied that she knew that but she wanted to see him in his coffin.

Mary Bell celebrated her eleventh birthday on 26 May and on the following day staff at the local nursery school reported for work to find that the place had been vandalised. There was a large hole in the slate roof and the intruder(s) had left a mess of overturned desks, spilled paint and torn books. Among the chaos, police found four notes, written either by a child or by a poorly-educated adult. The first two read: 'I murder so that I may come back', 'F*** off, we murder, watch out Fanny and Faggot'. The third was longer 'You are mice (cowardly, stupid) Y becurse we murdered Martin Go Brown, you Bete Look there are Murders about by Fanny and auld Faggot you Screws.' While the final note said simply 'We did murder Martin Brown F***of you Bastard' (original spellings retained.)

Although it wasn't spotted at the time, on the same day, Mary went to school as usual and wrote in her school diary:'…there were crowds of people beside an old house. I asked what was the matter, there has been a boy who just lay down and died.' Ominously, Mary's writing was accompanied by a drawing, which showed a boy lying on his back, a bottle and something that was clearly labelled 'tablet' on the floor beside him. In Mary's drawing, a workman with a pick axe was bending over the child's body.

In the wake of the attack on their premises, the nursery school had fitted an alarm system that was linked to the local police station and, when it sounded less than a week later, the police rushed to the scene and caught the culprits red-handed. They were Mary and

Norma, who were arrested and charged, before being bailed to appear at the juvenile court at a later date.

On 31 July 1968, three-year-old Brian Edward Howe failed to return home, having been out playing with Mary, Norma, one of his brothers and his dog. Seeing relatives and neighbours searching for the little boy, Mary and Norma latched on to Brian's teenage sister, offering to help her to look for him. By a roundabout route, they led Pat Howe to a former industrial site, known locally as 'The Tin Lizzie', now abandoned and littered with rusted machinery and old cars. Mary pointed out some concrete blocks and suggested that Brian might be playing near them.

'I don't think Brian goes there' Pat replied, returning to join the search party.

Brian's grass and weed covered body was found by the police among the concrete blocks shortly after eleven o'clock that night. The little boy's lips were blue and spotted with foam. His thighs were peppered with puncture wounds, some of his hair had been chopped off and his genitals had been partially skinned, possibly with a pair of broken scissors that lay on the ground nearby. Beneath his clothes, a letter 'M' had been carved into his stomach, possibly starting out as the letter 'N', to which an extra downward slash was added. Yet while a post-mortem examination confirmed that the cause of Brian's death was strangulation, pathologist Dr Bernard Tomlinson was able to tell the police that very little pressure had been applied to the child's throat. Not only that, but all Brian's injuries were shallow, suggesting that they had been inflicted without the use of great force. The pathologist advanced the theory that Brian had been murdered by another child.

The police brought in more than a hundred officers and cancelled all leave. Their first action was to draft a questionnaire, which was handed out to all of the area's children, aged between three and fifteen, asking them to describe their actions and whereabouts on the day of the murder. From one thousand two hundred completed questionnaires, the police selected sixty children to be interviewed in person, among them Norma and Mary, who had been seen with Brian shortly before his death.

Both Mary and Norma denied having been with Brian after midday. Then Mary suddenly recalled having seen another boy with Brian on the day of his death. She told the police that this boy hit Brian and had a pair of broken scissors, which she described in great detail. Unfortunately for Mary, the police had held back certain information and the existence of the broken scissors was known only to the investigating officers. Furthermore, the boy whom Mary named as Brian's companion had an unshakeable alibi that was confirmed by several other reliable witnesses.

Mary and Norma's vague and evasive responses to the police questions aroused great suspicion, which was heightened by their behaviour at Brian's funeral. Chief Inspector James Dobson looked on as Mary stood outside Brian's house, watching as the coffin containing his body emerged onto the street. She was laughing and rubbing her hands gleefully and Dobson's first thought was 'I've got to bring her in or she'll do another one.'

An interview with Norma Bell seemed to implicate Mary in Brian's murder. Norma claimed that Mary took her to the concrete blocks and showed her Brian's body, adding that Mary grasped her throat and squeezed it to demonstrate precisely how she had killed the little boy. Norma showed detectives the razor blade thought to have been used to carve the letter 'M' and was able to describe Brian's other wounds and draw an accurate picture of the position in which he was found. Finally, when Norma was shown eight pairs of broken scissors and asked to point out the ones that were lying near the body, she immediately picked the correct pair.

Although it was after midnight, the police went straight to Mary's house and, overriding the girl's father's objections, insisted on taking her to the police station for further questioning. Instantly awake, Mary saw the interrogation almost as a game.

While Mary and Norma gave apparently accurate accounts of the circumstances of Brian's murder, each blamed the other for causing the little boy's death. Chief Inspector Dobson now strongly believed that one or both girls had also killed Martin Brown and submitted samples of their handwriting for analysis; it was found to match the notes left at the vandalised nursery school. By that time, the police had traced a witness who had actually seen Brian being killed – a nine-year-old boy, who had the mental age of a four-year-old.

Told that she was to be arrested for Brian's murder, Mary cheekily replied 'That's all right with me.' Norma on the other hand became quite upset and shouted hysterically 'I never. I never.'

The two girls were tried together at the Newcastle upon Tyne Assizes before Mr Justice Cusack. The counsel for the prosecution was Rudolph Lyons Q.C., who opened the case by claiming that the killings were done solely for the pleasure and excitement they afforded the two defendants. In interviews with the police, both girls admitted to having been present but each blamed the actual murders on the other, giving detailed statements about what actually took place. Yet forensic evidence showed that fibres from clothes worn by both girls were recovered from the bodies. 'It was a joint enterprise' Lyons insisted.

Acting for Norma, defence counsel Mr R.P.S. Smith Q.C. admitted that both girls had lied but stated that he firmly believed that the evidence pointed to Mary as the most likely killer. 'There are a number of proved wicked lies that Mary has told. There are lies that Norma has told, no doubt to try and get herself out of trouble.

But the really wicked lies have been by Mary, trying to get somebody else into trouble.'

The trial was to last for nine days, during which Norma seemed distraught. She cried and fidgeted restlessly, looking round for sympathy and appeared to daydream. She herself gave evidence for five hours, during which she told the court that Mary had shown her how little boys or girls could be killed. She testified that Mary had told her that she meant to kill Brian and, when asked if she helped, insisted 'I never touched him.'

By contrast, Mary appeared alert, following the proceedings intelligently and seemingly without emotion, occasionally placing her fingers in her mouth. Almost as if she were enjoying sparring with the counsels, she remained composed as she gave her evidence, the majority of which involved trying to implicate Norma in the two killings. During her three and three quarter hours in the witness box, she stated that Norma had attacked and killed Brian, while she just stood and watched. 'I couldn't move. It was as though some glue was pulling me down' she explained, saying that she had tried to pull Norma off Brian but '…she just screamed and went mad.'

It emerged that Mary's mother Betty was a prostitute, said to have specialised in sadomasochistic practices, while her supposed father, Billy, was a petty criminal and a drunkard. As the court case unfolded, Mary's mother frequently disrupted the proceedings with her wailing and sobbing. Her face caked with smeared make up, she wore a badly fitting blonde wig and, more than once, she stormed out of the court, invariably re-entering a short while later. Once, she was heard to remark 'Jesus was only nailed to the cross – I am being hammered.' (At the conclusion of the trial, Betty Bell offered to sell her daughter's story to the press, but was turned down.) Before Mary was four years old, she had suffered numerous 'accidents' including drug overdoses and falls from windows, which all necessitated hospital treatment. It was suggested that the overdoses had been deliberately administered by her mother, whose first words on giving birth to Mary were said to have been 'Take that thing away from me.'

The issues that the jury needed to decide was whether the two girls were 'evil monsters' or whether they were simply damaged little girls, who were suffering from some form of psychiatric illness. As the trial progressed, it became evident to all concerned that Mary Bell was abnormal and that, in spite of her denials, she had strangled the two little boys. Psychiatrists appointed to assess her came to the conclusion that she was '…most abnormal, aggressive, vicious, cruel and incapable of remorse.' Dr Dan Orton told the court 'I've seen a lot of psychopathic children but I've never met one as intelligent, as manipulative or as dangerous as Mary.' Dr David Westbury, consultant psychiatrist to the Home Office' agreed that Mary was abnormally intelligent but, at the same time, a manipulative, violent and extremely dangerous bully, who would automatically lie to deny her violent behaviour. It was agreed that Norma was a rather 'backward' girl, of subnormal intelligence, whereas Mary had a '…dominating personality, with a somewhat unusual intelligence and a degree of cunning that is almost terrifying.' Dr Ian Frazer, the psychiatrist at the hospital where Norma had been staying since her arrest, told the court that Norma had a mental age of eight years and ten months. During her time at the hospital, she had never shown any signs of aggression and, although her capacity for knowing right from wrong was limited, she was capable of understanding that it was wrong to kill.

Witnesses testified that Mary was known for her erratic, violent outbursts and many of the local children were afraid of her. She had a sadistic streak, along with a habit of putting her hands round children's throats and throttling them and admitted that she enjoyed inflicting pain, Two weeks before Martin Brown's death, Mary and Flora took a three-year-old boy to buy sweets. 'John G.' was later found alone dazed and bleeding and, although the police and an ambulance were called, no action was taken against the girls. The following day, a mother complained to the police that Mary and Norma had tried to strangle her daughter Pauline Watson while she was playing in a sandpit with three of her friends. Although Mrs Watson claimed that there were clearly visible marks on Pauline's neck, beyond the police warning Mary and Norma about their conduct, nothing else was done, mainly because Pauline was too afraid of Mary to tell the whole truth about what had happened. Norma's parents also complained that Mary had attacked and throttled one of Norma's sisters, stating that Norma's father had to hit Mary hard on the shoulder to get her to release her vice-like grip on his daughter's throat. One of the last witnesses to testify was twelve-year-old David McReady, who stated that, after Martin Brown's death, Mary had once pointed to the house where he was found and boasted 'I am a murderer'.

In his closing speech, the counsel for the prosecution described Mary as a 'fiend', while painting Norma as a child of low intelligence who fell victim to Mary's '…evil and compelling influence.'

'It is very easy to revile a little girl…without pausing to ponder how the whole story came about' countered Mary's defence counsel, Mr J. Harvey Robson.

The jury debated for three hours and forty minutes before finding Norma Bell not guilty of murder or manslaughter. She was later given three years' probation for her part in the break-in at the nursery and placed under psychiatric supervision. For Mary Bell, the jury's deliberations had a different outcome – she was found not guilty of murder, since it was felt that she was suffering from diminished responsibility at the time of the killings. However, she was found guilty on two counts of manslaughter, at which she burst into tears.

Mr Justice Cusack described Mary as 'dangerous', adding that there was a very grave risk to other children if she was not closely watched. Yet, having sentenced Mary to detention for life, the judge then struggled to know exactly what to do with her. 'I should be willing to make a hospital order under Section 60 of the Mental Health Act, so that she could be taken to a mental institution to receive treatment, combined with a restriction order, unrestricted in point of time, so that she could not be released without special procedure and the authority of the Secretary of State' he stated, continuing' Unhappily, I am unable to make such an order because one of the requirements of the Mental Health Act is that I must be satisfied that there is a hospital to which she can go and be admitted to that institution within twenty-eight days.'

Cusack summoned Home Office Psychiatrist Dr David Westbury, who stated that Mary had a psychiatric disorder within the meaning of the Mental Health Act. Asked by the judge if he knew of any place where Mary could be sent, Westbury replied that he didn't, adding that the matter was the responsibility of the health department of the Ministry of Social Security.

'It is an appalling thing that, with a child as young as this one, one has to take into consideration such matters. I am not entirely unsympathetic but anxious as I am to do everything for her benefit, my primary duty is to protect other people' concluded Cusack.

Whereas Mary needed treatment for her psychiatric illness, none of the existing homes for disturbed children offered the necessary security stipulated by the judge, while none of the more secure facilities could provide her with the right social setting essential for her recovery. She was eventually sent to Red Bank Approved School in Newton-Le-Willows until shortly after her seventeenth birthday, when she was transferred to Styal Prison, in Cheshire. After this move, the headmaster of Red Bank publicly spoke out, claiming that the prison environment was undoing the progress she had made at the school. However, with Mary the only female in-patient among more than two hundred boys at Red Bank, after claims that she was at the centre of a sex and pornography scandal, it was felt that a move to a woman's prison was the most appropriate course of action.

In 1977, Mary was transferred to an open prison in Staffordshire, from which she promptly absconded with another inmate. The police reassured the public that Mary was not a dangerous killer '…just a missing twenty-year-old from an open prison.' She was recaptured three days later.

Askham Grange Prison (author's collection)

In 1980, twenty-three-year-old Mary was released from Askham Grange Open Prison, having already spent several weeks working as a waitress in a café near York Minster. After having one abortion, she gave birth to a daughter in 1984 and, although the child was made a ward of court, she was allowed to keep the baby and bring her up.

In 1998, Mary collaborated with author Gitta Sereny on a book about her crimes. Having been given a new identity on her release, on publication of the book journalists purloined Ms Sereny's telephone bills and Mary's cover was blown. Faced with harassment from the press, Mary was forced into hiding and had to reveal her true identity to her then teenage daughter.

In 2003, a High Court judge decreed that the identities of Mary Bell and her daughter should be kept secret, her right to privacy and family life judged to outweigh the freedom of the press. In 2009, this order was extended to include Mary's first grandchild.

Note: Although this is the most recent case covered in this collection, while there is a wealth of conflicting information available on the internet, because of the age of the defendants many of the contemporary newspaper reports are purposely lacking in detail. There are considerable variations among those that do exist. For example, some reports state that it was Mary and Norma who alerted the workmen to the presence of Martin's body in the derelict house. I have tried to make sure that all of the 'facts' as I have written them above have appeared in at least two independent sources to give the most accurate account possible of the case.

Bibliography (Newspapers):

Birmingham Daily Post

Blackburn Standard

Bradford Observer

Caledonian Mercury

Carlisle Journal

Cheshire Observer

Coventry Standard

Daily Mail

Daily News

Gloucester Citizen

Gloucestershire Echo

Grantham Journal

Hertford Mercury and Reformer

Huddersfield Daily Chronicle

Hull Packet

Ipswich Journal

Leeds and Yorkshire Mercury

Lichfield Mercury

Lincolnshire Chronicle

Liverpool Mercury

Lloyd's Weekly Newspaper

Manchester Courier and Lancashire General Advertiser

Northampton Mercury

Nottingham Evening Post

Portsmouth Evening News

Reading Mercury

Reynolds's Newspaper

Sheffield Independent

The Devon and Exeter Daily Gazette

The Manchester Guardian

The Scotsman

The Stamford Mercury

The Times

The Western Gazette

The Western Mail

Westmorland Gazette & Kendal Advertiser

Yorkshire Evening Post

Printed in Great Britain
by Amazon